ANGEL
NUMBERS

Also by Doreen Virtue, Ph.D.

CD Programmes

ANGEL MEDICINE: A Healing Meditation CD

ANGELS AMONG US (with Michael Toms)

MESSAGES FROM YOUR ANGELS
(abridged audio book)

PAST-LIFE REGRESSION WITH THE ANGELS

DIVINE PRESCRIPTIONS

THE ROMANCE ANGELS

CONNECTING WITH YOUR ANGELS

MANIFESTING WITH THE ANGELS

KARMA RELEASING

HEALING YOUR APPETITE, HEALING YOUR LIFE

HEALING WITH THE ANGELS

DIVINE GUIDANCE

CHAKRA CLEARING

Oracle Cards
(44 or 45 divination cards and guidebook)

HEALING WITH THE ANGELS ORACLE CARDS

HEALING WITH THE FAIRIES ORACLE CARDS

MESSAGES FROM YOUR ANGELS ORACLE CARDS
(card deck and booklet)

*MAGICAL MERMAIDS AND DOLPHINS
ORACLE CARDS* (card deck and booklet)

ARCHANGEL ORACLE CARDS
(card deck and booklet)

GODDESS GUIDANCE ORACLE CARDS
(card deck and booklet)

MAGICAL UNICORNS ORACLE CARDS

SAINTS AND ANGELS ORACLE CARDS
(available in 2006)

All of the above are available at your local book-shop, or may be ordered by calling Hay House Publishers on 020 8962 1230.

Hay House UK: **www.hayhouse.co.uk**
Hay House USA: **www.hayhouse.com**
Hay House Australia: **www.hayhouse.com.au**
Hay House South Africa: **orders@psdprom.co.za**

Doreen's Website: **www.AngelTherapy.com**

❀ ❀ ❀

ALSO BY LYNNETTE BROWN

CHAKRA ENERGY ORACLE CARDS

Lynnette's Website:
www.angelicwonders.com

❀ ❀ ❀

ANGEL NUMBERS

The Angels Explain the Meaning of
111, 444, and Other Numbers in Your Life

Doreen Virtue, PhD,
and Lynnette Brown

HAY HOUSE
Australia • Canada • Hong Kong
South Africa • United Kingdom • United States

First published and distributed in the United Kingdom by Hay House UK Ltd, Unit 62, Canalot Studios, 222 Kensal Rd, London W10 5BN. Tel.: (44) 20 8962 1230; Fax: (44) 20 8962 1239. www.hayhouse.co.uk

Published and distributed in the United States of America by Hay House, Inc., PO Box 5100, Carlsbad, CA 92018-5100. Tel.: (760) 431 7695 or (800) 654 5126; Fax: (760) 431 6948 or (800) 650 5115. www.hayhouse.com

Published and distributed in Australia by Hay House Australia Ltd, 18/36 Ralph St, Alexandria NSW 2015. Tel.: 612 9669 4299; Fax: 612 9669 4144. www.hayhouse.com.au

Published and distributed in the Republic of South Africa by Hay House SA (Pty), Ltd, PO Box 990, Witkoppen 2068. Tel./Fax: 2711-706 6612. orders@psdprom.co.za

Distributed in Canada by Raincoast, 9050 Shaughnessy St, Vancouver, BC V6P 6E5. Tel.: (604) 323 7100; Fax: (604) 323 2600

The authors of this book does not dispense medical advice or prescribe the use of any technique as a form of treatment for physical or medical problems without the advice of a physician, either directly or indirectly. The intent of the author is only to offer information of a general nature to help you in your quest for emotional and spiritual wellbeing. In the event you use any of the information in this book for yourself, which is your constitutional right, the authors and the publisher assume no responsibility for your actions.

A catalogue record for this book is available from the British Library.

ISBN 1-4019-0515-3

Editorial supervision: Jill Kramer

Design: Amy Gingery

Printed and bound in Great Britain by Butler & Tanner Ltd

CONTENTS

AN INTRODUCTION
TO ANGEL NUMBERS

Y ou have guardian angels with you right now—continuously—guaranteed! Your angels guide you through your thoughts, feelings, words, and visions. They also show you signs—that is, things that you see repeatedly with your physical eyes. One of their favorite signs relates to number sequences. These are numerals that you repeatedly see on license plates, phone numbers, clocks, and so on.

Doreen: If you've ever wondered about the significance of these number sequences, you're not alone. Many people have asked me about their meaning during my angel workshops. So,

I went to the Source and asked for guidance to interpret the meanings of repetitive number sequences. A longtime student of Pythagorean sacred numerology (including a past life as his student) and also an angel channeler, I rapidly received information as to what the angels were conveying through these sequences.

My workshop audiences loved it when I discussed the significance of these groups of numbers, and asked if I would compile a list for them to refer to. So, my book *Healing with the Angels* includes a chapter listing the meanings. After *Healing with the Angels'* publication, many people said that they carried the book with them as a reference tool for interpreting the numbers they saw. They asked me to create an even more comprehensive book that was pocket-size. You now hold the results of those requests in your hands.

Lynnette: When Doreen invited me to work with her on this venture, I accepted gratefully and understood that this was an important assignment. I traveled to a very special place, Hawaii, which is home to my soul, in order to connect with God, the angels, and ascended masters while working on this extensive list. I was guided to do most of the channeling work in some of the sacred spaces of the island—namely, Honaunau (often called the city of refuge); the Paleaku Garden Peace Sanctuary; the Kilauea volcano; and in the beautiful ocean while swimming with the dolphins, whales, and other incredible sea life.

Through prayer, meditation, and studies with God, the angels, and the ascended masters, I learned that these number sequences revealed additional information, which I used in my spiritual counseling practice. I found that the numbers I saw around my clients acted as portals through which I could retrieve specific Divine guidance. This guidance, which sprang from the sacred numbers, has had profound healing effects upon my clients.

Many of them have told me that as they recognize and interpret the numbers around them, they feel more connected to the angels and God. This connection allows them to open the door to an incredible connection that brings them peace, hope, and love. Understanding and using angelic numerology has helped me receive more detailed and in-depth messages for myself and my clients.

Doreen and Lynnette: We made this book small and portable so that you can easily carry it with you. After all, angels give us number messages while we're driving, on airplanes, at work, and at home.

Number-sequence interpretation is an easy way to receive messages from your angels. Numerals are everywhere, from digital clocks to billboards to license plates. Each number has a unique vibrational frequency relating directly to its meaning.

This ancient wisdom harkens back to great teachers such as Hermes, Plato, and Pythagoras. Pythagoras said that everything in the Universe is mathematically precise, and that each number has its own vibration, meaning, and virtue. Plato wrote that everything in the Universe is built from basic geometrical shapes derived from numbers, such as triangles (from 3) and cubes (from 4). The sacred mystical Jewish text of the *Zohar* (*Kabbalah*) discusses the power of the vibrations from numbers and letters.

The angels also say that the placement of the numbers in a sequence holds special meaning. For example, when there are three or more numbers, the center digit is of primary focus. The angels say that this number represents the "heart" of the matter.

Numerology is one of the few sacred sciences that has kept its magic from ancient to modern times. The angels remind us that we're all alchemists, powerful enough to manifest our true desires through Divine magic. Numbers point out the importance of seeing Heavenly messages third-dimensionally in order to show us the lessons, growth opportunities, and guidance contained within each experience.

How to Use This Book

When you see a number sequence (especially more than once in a short span of time), look up its interpretation in this book. In addition to reading the message, listen to your own angels' guidance that comes through your thoughts, feelings, and visions. Ask your angels for clarification if the message is unclear by saying to them silently or aloud, "Please clearly explain so I'll easily understand." As with any divination tool, defer to your own inner wisdom as the ultimate authority. In other words, if in doubt, trust your gut.

— Interpreting longer number sequences. This book provides the general meaning of numbers 00 to 999. For larger number sequences, you can read the meaning of the first three-digit part of the sequence in this book, and then "add" the second or third sections of the number.

— Four-digit numbers. To interpret the meaning of four-digit numbers, break the number sequence into three digits and read that interpretation. Then, add the last digit's interpretation to know the meaning of the entire sequence. For instance, to interpret 2048, begin with the first three digits: 204, and read its interpretation in this book:

204

God and the angels ask for your patience. Stay filled with faith that your prayers have been heard and are answered.

Then, read the interpretation of the last of the four digits in 2048, which is 8:

8

Financial abundance is coming to you now.

Put these two interpretations together and you have the meaning of 2048: *God and the angels ask for your patience. Stay filled with faith that your prayers have been heard and are answered. Financial abundance is coming to you now.*

Summarizing these combined interpretations, then, 2048 means: *Heaven assures you that your money needs will be supplied. Have patience.*

— **Five-digit numbers**. You can interpret five-digit numbers in a similar fashion. Just take the first three digits and read its meaning in this book. Then, read the interpretation of the last two digits in the number sequence. Combine the meanings and summarize them.

Here's an example using the five-digit number sequence, 99900:

999

Get to work, Lightworker! The world needs your Divine life purpose right now. Fully embark upon your sacred mission without delay or hesitation.

And here is the meaning of the last two numbers:

00

This means that the Creator is emphasizing a message to you and asks that you pay attention and follow the guidance without delay.

Next, add the meanings of the two together to find that 99900 means:

Get to work, Lightworker! The world needs your Divine life purpose right now. Fully embark upon your sacred mission without delay or hesitation. The Creator is emphasizing this message to you and asks that you pay attention and follow the guidance without delay.

In other words, God wants you to fully commit to your life's purpose . . . *now!*

— **Six-digit** numbers. To interpret the meaning of a six-digit number such as 225496, you'd break it into two- or three-digit components. In this case, we'll break it into 225 and 496. Then, read the interpretation for the first section, which is:

225

Trust that this change is for the best. You're in a period of transition—letting go of the past and that which is no longer working. Let go and move forward with confidence and faith.

Then, you'd look up the meaning of the second three-digit segment:

496

The angels ask you to make your Divine life mission your top priority right now. Don't worry about how it will come about, or any other material aspect concerning your purpose. The angels help with everything.

Next, compile the meanings of each segment so that 225496 means:

Trust that this change is for the best. You're in a period of transition—letting go of the past and that which is no longer working. Let go and move forward with confidence and faith. The angels ask you to make your Divine life mission your top priority right now. Don't worry about how it will come about, or any other material aspect concerning your purpose. The angels help with everything.

This is a message, in summary, that says, *Have faith in the changes you're experiencing. The angels ask you to focus on your Divine life mission, and they'll supply all your material needs.*

— **Number sequences with personal meanings.** You may also notice number sequences that signify things of personal significance, such as birth dates, anniversaries, telephone numbers, and such. In these cases, the angels are giving you an even deeper message. First, think of the person connected with that particular numeral (for example, when you see a friend's birth date). Then, ask your angels for additional information related to the message. Listen to the impressions that enter your thoughts and body. For additional information related to the message, read this book's interpretation connected to that number sequence.

— **The number 3 and the ascended masters.** The number 3 refers to ascended masters, great spiritual teachers who once walked upon the earth, as well as various religions' deities.

Doreen: When I give an angel-number reading for someone who sees the numeral 3 frequently, I usually find that Jesus is with that person. However, in some cases, a 3 can signify the presence of other ascended masters from other spiritual traditions, including saints, Bodhisattvas, and divinities. The numeral 3 can also signify a goddess's presence, especially when the 3 follows a 1 in a 13 arrangement. That's because 13 relates to the annual number of moon cycles, and the moon is associated with feminine spirituality.

You'll attract the presence and help of ascended masters who mirror your beliefs and religion. That's why Christians have Jesus with them, while Hindus are more apt to be accompanied by Ganesh. You can also ask ascended masters to be with you; and to guide, protect, and heal you. I find that people who frequently pray to and communicate with the ascended masters are those who see the most 3's in number sequences.

✦✦✦

Doreen and Lynnette: You'll love the continual conversations you'll engage in with Spirit, with the help of the interpretations you'll find in this book. Once you begin interpreting the number sequences, you'll discover spiritual signs and messages everywhere you go. The more you learn about and notice number sequences, the more you'll realize that Heaven is always with you—speaking with you, guiding you, and loving you.

❂ ❂ ❂ ❂ ❂ ❂

THE GENERAL
MEANING OF THE NUMBERS

00

The Creator is emphasizing this message to you and asks that you pay attention and follow the guidance without delay.

0

Zero relates to prayer or meditation practice, and the all-encompassing God Source. God is talking to you.

1

This is a binary number; every number is divisible by one. We are all one, thereby we're all associated by thought. Watch your thoughts, and focus on your desires rather than your fears.

2

Have faith and courage. Your prayers are manifesting, even if they aren't visible yet.

3

The ascended masters (such as Jesus) are near. They've responded to your prayers and want to help you.

4

Angels are with you. Call upon them for help, guidance, and feelings of love and security.

5

This number relates to change, transformation, transmutation, and alchemy. Something in your life is changing, or about to change, for the better.

6

The number 6 relates to earthly materials, such as possessions, planetary issues, and concrete tangibles. Be careful to balance thoughts or worries about the material with a focus and faith in the spiritual.

7

You're on the right path. Keep up the good work!

8

Financial abundance is coming to you now.

9

Your Divine life purpose involves the giving of service through your natural talents, passions, and interests.

10

You're receiving Divine guidance from God through thoughts, ideas, insights, or what's called *claircognizance* (knowing facts without knowing how you received the information). Stay positive about the messages you receive.

11

Pay attention to your repetitive thoughts and ideas, as they're answers to your prayers. This number also signifies a highly creative person who needs to avoid addictive behaviors.

12

Have faith that Spirit is speaking to you through repetitive thoughts, ideas, and insights that guide you to improve something in your life, or the life of others. Allow your positive affirmations to lead the way.

13

Ascended masters ask you to stay positive and give them any fears or doubts that they can heal and transmute. This number also means the sacred feminine, the goddess, and the intuitive side, as there are 13 moon cycles in a year.

14

Angels are helping you manifest your positive thoughts, affirmations, and visualizations into reality.

15

Change and elevate your thoughts. Use affirmations and prayers to help your thoughts and feelings rise above negativity.

16

Your thoughts create your reality, so only hold positive thoughts and expectations about material issues, and all your needs are met.

17

You're on the right path with your thoughts. You have good reason to be optimistic about your plans and path. This powerful and sacred number also represents the holy Trinity and pyramids.

18

Think only thoughts of abundance and prosperity, as your thoughts are manifesting very quickly right now.

19

Keep your mind focused on helping yourself and others lead healthier and more peaceful lives. Stay positive and optimistic about your Divine life mission.

20

The Creator asks you to have faith. Even if you can't see the results of your prayers and actions right now, trust that they're bearing wonderful fruit for you.

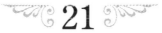

21

Keep the faith and stay positive! Allow your affirmations to support you.

22

Your deep conviction manifests miracles and wonderful new opportunities. Keep the faith!

23

The ascended masters are helping you keep the faith. They're with you right now, and are available to you as you ask for their assistance.

24

The angels are helping you keep the faith and have courage. They want you to know that they're with you right now. Believe in your angels, and believe in their desire and power to help you.

25

Have faith that your life is changing for the best. You and your loved ones are safe and protected throughout these changes.

26

Have faith that all your earthly needs are met, now and in the future. Give any material concerns to Spirit, and follow the Divine guidance that compels you to take action.

27

Continue on your path with faith. You're doing the right thing, so keep up the good work.

28

Have faith in the abundance of the Universe. Prosperity is materializing for you as you continue to persevere.

29

Have faith in yourself and your Divine life purpose. You're qualified, ready, and prepared to help others!

30

God and the ascended masters are here to help you. Call upon them for help with anything that brings you and your loved ones peace, and anything that helps you on your life path.

31

The ascended masters are helping you shift your thoughts to the empowering level of love and peace.

32

Keep believing in your connection with the ascended masters. As you turn to them with increasing frequency, so shall your faith in this connection grow.

33

Many ascended masters surround you and assist you in all ways. They've come to help you with your mission and to answer your prayers. Tune to them now, and ask them any question you wish.

34

Ascended masters and angels are here with you. Talk to them frequently about your feelings and thoughts, and listen to their replies, which come to you as repetitive impressions, signs, and inner signals.

35

The ascended masters are asking you to make changes to increase your spiritual awareness and power. Team up with these loving and powerful masters to heal, or to help you release those parts of your life that are no longer serving you and the Light.

36

The ascended masters want to help you with your material life, especially by providing you with support for your life mission and your loved ones. The ascended masters ask you to keep your mind focused on Spirit and not to unduly focus on the material world.

37

You are Divinely guided on the right track by the ascended masters. Turn to them during meditation and prayers for guidance, answers, and reassurance. The ascended masters are pleased with the path you've chosen, and they want to help you.

38

Increased abundance is coming your way, and the ascended masters wish to reassure you about financial support in your life. Notice and follow the repetitive messages they give you through your thoughts, feelings, words, and visions.

39

The ascended masters say, "Get to work, Lightworker!" Your mission is much needed, and they wish to help you along your path. Don't delay in devoting yourself to the completion of important tasks related to your life purpose.

40

God and the angels want you to know that they're with you, guiding you every step of the way. Take their loving hands and allow yourself to be supported.

41

The angels say, "Watch your thoughts, and only think about love and success. In this way, only love and success come into your life." The angels are available to help you choose positive thoughts as you call upon them for help.

42

Your angels ask you to keep the faith that your prayers have been heard and are answered. If you need to, ask the angels to increase the level of your faith.

43

Angels and ascended masters are with you, supporting and loving you. Mentally talk to them about your hopes, dreams, or fears, and ask them to help you. They always come to your aid when invoked.

44

Many angels are with you now. You can ask these angels to help you with anything that brings peace to you and your loved ones. Don't *tell* the angels how to fix a situation; just ask them to fix it. The Divine and infinite wisdom of the Creator guides you (through the angels) to a wonderfully ingenious solution.

45

The angels ask you to make necessary life changes without delay. You already know what those changes are. Ask the angels to help you find the courage and strength to make them, and know that these changes ultimately benefit everyone.

46

The angels want to help you with your material needs, especially as they're related to your life mission and your loved ones. They can help you with anything small or large that brings you and your loved ones peace. Just ask them for help.

47

The angels say that you're doing a good job and that you're on the right path. They want you to know that they're with you every step of the way, and they can help you even more as you call upon them for specific help.

48

"Angels of Abundance" are with you. Know that there is an-infinite supply, and that lack is just an illusion. More money is coming to you now, so don't worry about your finances.

49

The angels ask you to get to work on your Divine mission without delay. Now is the time to finish any incomplete projects. Clear the space in your calendar to work on your true priorities.

50

God and the spirit world are urging you to make this change. They ensure that the transition is harmonious and that you and your loved ones are supported in all ways. Let go, and let God help you during this time of change.

51

Keep your thoughts focused on a positive outcome during this time of life change. Even though you may not be entirely sure what your future holds, you can be sure that things are improving. Stay positive about your intentions and goals.

52

Change is the only thing that's constant. Trust in this truth, and don't fear the changes you're making and experiencing. As one door closes, another one opens for the better.

53

The ascended masters are assisting you by clearing the path for this change. Call upon their loving power to ensure your continued smooth transition.

54

The angels assure you that the change you're contemplating or experiencing is for the best. They're with you right now and continue to support you during this time of transition. Call upon them frequently.

55

Buckle your seat belt, as you're going through (or about to go through) a major positive life change. It's time to let go of that which is no longer working, and allow it to be healed or replaced with something better.

56

As you go through this important and much-needed life change, you receive new blessings and opportunities. All your needs are met during this time of transition.

57

This change is leading you upon your Divine path—trust that everything is on the upswing, even if you can't actually see the outcome yet.

58

Your financial situation is changing for the better. Call upon the "Angels of Abundance" for support, help, and guidance about finances, and be sure to follow their lead on using money and handling debt wisely.

59

Your life is becoming more stable, and you're now getting a clearer picture of your life path. Embrace it fully without delay, and dive right in, as this is the perfect time for you and your mission.

60

The Creator is helping you with your material concerns. You're reminded to seek first the kingdom of God, and all the rest is added unto you. Keep your heart and mind focused Heavenward, and know that your needs are always met.

61

Hold positive thoughts and expectations about your material needs so that you manifest a steady supply. Give any fears or worries to Spirit for healing and transmutation. Your thoughts are powerful, so guard them carefully and only focus upon your desires.

62

Have faith in this world. Keep believing that people are essentially good, even when they appear otherwise. Be assured that the Universe supports you materially, now and always.

63

The ascended masters (such as Jesus) are helping you in earthly matters. You can also help Earth's ascension into the golden age through your prayers, affirmations, and Divine light energy.

64

Celestial and earthly angels are helping you with material support. They're making sure that your needs are met, especially as you focus on your spiritual path. The more gratitude you hold toward the angels, the more you open the flow of support.

65

Look for a change in your life relating to material issues, perhaps a move or a new job. This is a change for the better, even if it's uncomfortable at first.

66

Keep your thoughts focused Heavenward during this time, and avoid excessive worry or obsession with materiality.

67

You're balanced with respect to your path of service and material issues. You're applying your spiritual wisdom to help Earth and her inhabitants. Keep up the good work!

68

You've materialized abundance. Keep the flow going by donating to causes you believe in. Keep your arms and grateful heart open to receiving. The more you allow yourself to receive, the more resources you have available with which to help others.

69

This number refers to balance, like the yin and yang. Balance your spiritual and material focus by spending time and energy on both. All your needs are met as you devote yourself fully to your Divine life purpose.

70

This is a message from the Creator that you're on the right path. Stay centered through prayer and meditation.

71

Keep up your positive thoughts and ideas. Don't allow other people or situations to sway you from your intentions.

72

Trust and continue on this path. Your optimism is well founded! The Kabbalists recognize 72 names of God, so this number can also validate and elevate your clear connection with the Creator.

73

The ascended masters say that you're on the right path, and they're helping you every step of the way. Ask them for any additional assistance that you may need.

74

The angels say that your choice is a good one. Continue along the path that you've started, and call upon your angels if you ever feel yourself wavering.

75

This change is for the better. You made the right decision, even if you don't know the final outcome yet. Keep going!

76

You're on the right path, and your material needs are supplied now and in the future. Give any earthly concerns to Spirit, and be open to receiving.

77

Congratulations! You're on the right path mentally and physically. Stick to your intentions and stand your ground.

78

You're on the right path, moving toward abundance and prosperity in all ways. As you sow, so shall you reap. You've been listening to your true inner guidance, and putting energy and effort in that direction. Now you're enjoying the rewards of your right action.

79

You've devoted yourself to giving sacred service through your Divine life purpose, and you're taking the right course of action toward the fruition of this mission.

80

The Creator is bestowing great abundance upon you—not as a reward so much, but through the Divine law of cause and effect. Because you've been working on a prosperity program with guidance from the Light, it is more able to shine support upon you.

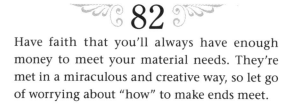

81

Keep your thoughts positively focused on the area of prosperity and abundance. Stay confident and peaceful, and know that the Source of all is within you. You're in a place right now where your thoughts about money are manifesting instantly.

82

Have faith that you'll always have enough money to meet your material needs. They're met in a miraculous and creative way, so let go of worrying about "how" to make ends meet.

83

Your abundance is accelerated by your spiritual connections with the ascended masters. Pray to, and meditate upon, these masters, who are guiding your path and helping you experience an uninterrupted flow in your life.

84

The angels are helping your finances flow more abundantly. Call upon the "Angels of Abundance" at any time for advice, and guidance with money matters.

85

Your financial flow is steadily increasing and improving. Stay centered in gratitude, and be willing to both give and receive with joy in your heart.

86

Give any material concerns to Spirit, as Heaven is giving you a new windfall of abundance. Be alert to noticing and receiving the bountiful gifts and blessings coming your way.

87

The path you're on supports the flow of your abundance. You're on a roll in many ways, and have "struck gold" by tuning in to and following your innermost guidance. You're now realizing the secret of giving and receiving.

88

Great abundance is yours. Prosperity is flowing to you in ever-increasing amounts. Feel grateful, and be sure to pass along the flow to others as you feel guided.

89

Your Divine life mission is abundantly supported by the Universe in all ways.

90

God is supporting your sacred life purpose. Ask and you will always receive Divine guidance and help for your mission.

91

Watch your thoughts about your Lightwork and your life mission. Stay positive, and know that you're qualified and have enough power to heal and help others.

92

Have faith in yourself and your ability to fulfill your Divine life mission.

93

The ascended masters are here to help you with this project, especially as it relates to your Divine life mission.

94

The angels ask you to stay focused on bringing more love and light into your world through your sacred purpose.

95

The changes you're experiencing or considering are beneficial to your Divine purpose in life.

96

Dive right into your Divine purpose, and all of your needs are supplied and manifested along the way. You're ready now, and your mission is needed.

97

You're on the right path to fully manifesting your Divine life purpose. Keep going, and be open to giving and receiving love along the way.

98

As you fully devote yourself to your mission of light and love (which involves your natural talents, passions, and interests), money takes care of itself. Just focus on giving service, and you'll always have enough—with plenty to spare and share.

99

Get to work, Lightworker! Your Divine life mission is needed now more than ever, and any contribution you can make toward bringing more light and love to your world is imperative. The preparation for your life's work is complete for now.

100

Keep your thoughts totally aligned with God's love and light. Your positive thoughts and actions make a huge difference—especially right now.

101

Allow your thoughts to be centered and focused on God. Be creative, like the Creator. Know that you're helping with Heaven's plan as you keep your thoughts centered upon peace.

102

God and the Universal Wisdom are elevating your thoughts and helping you keep the faith in this situation. Ask God to help you heal away any doubts.

103

Your thoughts and intentions are supported by God and the ascended masters. Call upon them frequently to guide your actions and thoughts. They keep you focused on the Divine truth in all ways.

104

God and the angelic realm are supporting your positive thoughts. As you meditate upon Divine love, you feel the depth of their love for you. Keep your thoughts focused on love, and call upon Heaven to re-center you when needed.

105

Allow yourself to lean on God and Divine guidance for clarity regarding the changes you're experiencing or considering. Call upon God frequently for assistance in walking through these changes with grace and ease.

106

Your material desires come to you easily by manifesting with intentions of unconditional love and worthiness. Surrender any money or material worries to God, and trust that your needs are already taken care of.

107

The path of manifestation is through God, and by following your Divine guidance. You're on the right track; however, continue to devote time and energy to speaking and listening to Spirit to ensure your continued success.

108

Your beliefs and mind-set around God bring many forms of abundance to you. Like the Creator, you can share this wealth with others in many ways. Stay positive, and teach others to hold positive thoughts about material supply as well.

109

God is elevating your consciousness regarding your Divine life purpose. Stay mentally and emotionally connected to God for guidance, courage, and support regarding your purpose.

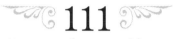

110

Keep your thoughts focused upon God and Divine love, as you're creating your reality with your thoughts and beliefs. Engage in creative activities, and avoid addictive behaviors.

111

An energetic gateway has opened for you, rapidly manifesting your thoughts into reality. Choose your thoughts wisely at this time, ensuring that they match your desires. Don't put any energy into thinking about fears at all, lest you manifest them.

112

Keep your thoughts buoyantly optimistic and hopeful, especially about your future. Have faith in your manifesting power.

113

The ascended masters, especially the goddesses, are helping to keep your thoughts positive and loving. Call upon them without delay if you have any negative thoughts or feelings, or are involved in any unpleasant situations.

114

Think like an angel, seeing the best within yourself, others, and every situation. In this way, you're a miracle maker!

115

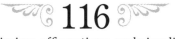

Your powerful intentions are guiding you through this time of transition. Stay positive and focused through these times of change.

116

Your optimism, affirmations, and visualizations create a steady flow of material supply. You have the power to manifest anything you need, now and in the future.

117

You're on the right path with your positive affirmations and intentions. You expect the best, so the best happens.

118

Your positive and optimistic thoughts and visualizations are manifesting waves of prosperity and abundance. Your receiving and giving are Divinely balanced.

119

Keep your thoughts and beliefs about your sacred life mission at a positive level. Expect success in everything you do, especially as it relates to your spiritual path and sacred mission.

120

God urges you to stay filled with faith and positive thoughts. Everything is working out for your highest good.

121

Keep the faith and stay positive, as your thoughts, feelings, and beliefs are manifesting into reality. Think only about your desires, and give any worries to Spirit for healing and transmutation.

122

Your thoughts and your faith are very sacred tools that you brought to Earth for this incarnation. This number sequence is a sign for you to honor these tools and know how powerful they are.

123

Simplify your life. Get rid of anything that's pulling at your energy, time, or finances—especially anything that pulls you away from your life purpose. The ascended masters are helping you with this simplification.

124

The angels are helping you stay strong with faith and a positive outlook. Call upon the angels for help with ideas, direction, and courage to work toward this aim.

125

Stay positive and optimistic about the changes you're experiencing or considering making. Your faith helps the transition to be smooth and harmonious.

126

You're manifesting the flow of your material supply. To increase the flow, increase your faith and positive thinking.

127

Have faith that your continued affirmations and positive thinking are working! You're manifesting at an ever-higher level.

128

You're a master creator and manifestor. Your flow of abundance is a direct reflection of your thoughts right now. You have the power to rapidly manifest with your thoughts.

129

Have faith, and stay positive about your Divine life mission and your ability to bring it to fruition. You're perfectly qualified for your mission. Just follow your inner guidance and affirm that all is well.

130

The feminine aspect of Creation is supporting you and your work right now. Be open to receiving, and notice your intuitive, feeling nature. Call upon the goddesses to assist you in staying positive. Get in tune with the moon cycles, and notice how they affect your emotions and manifestations as well.

131

The ascended masters—especially the goddesses—stand ready to assist you. They're communicating with you through thoughts and ideas.

132

The ascended masters, goddesses, and sacred feminine energy are elevating your consciousness to a level of perfect faith and positive thinking. Call upon them often to help you stay spiritually centered.

133

The ascended masters are supporting your healing work by helping you have positive thoughts, intentions, and affirmations. They're whispering Divinely guided ideas of love to you, so be sure to notice your musings and insights.

134

The angels and ascended masters are asking you to review your current thoughts about the sacred feminine, as well as female relationships. The goddesses and angels empower you as you call upon them.

135

A significant healing with female relationships is a welcome blessing, which is brought about by the positive thoughts and affirmations you've been working with lately. Keep affirming the goodness within yourself, your mother, and other important females in your life to heal and open you even more.

136

The ascended masters and goddesses are ensuring that your needs are continuously met. You help with this manifestation by keeping your thoughts attuned to the positive.

137

The goddesses are helping you keep up the path that you've undertaken. Lean on them for support. Know that it's okay for you to receive assistance from others.

138

You have many ascended masters—especially mother goddesses—helping you receive the bountiful supply of abundance they're giving you.

139

The ascended masters—especially the goddesses—are blessing and supporting your Divine life purpose. Call upon them for any answers or guidance you may need.

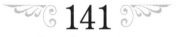

140

God and the angels are helping you hold positive thoughts and intentions. Take some quiet time for contemplation and meditation, and call upon Heaven for guidance.

141

Focus your thoughts and intentions on connecting with the angels. You need not force this process; just relax and breathe.

142

Your consistent work with positive intentions has helped you to clearly connect with the angelic realm. Have faith that your angels do hear you.

143

The angels and ascended masters urge you to maintain a positive viewpoint about yourself and your world. Ask them to help you stay in this frame of mind, if needed.

144

The Archangel Jophiel, along with the rest of the angelic realm, is assisting you with beautifying your thoughts. These positive thoughts are a major contribution to this world.

145

Your positive thoughts and affirmations are working in concert with your angels to bring about a positive change. As you go through this change, keep in steady contact with your angels through your prayers and meditations.

146

Your angels ask you to stay positive about your material life. Post affirmations around you so that you can see them regularly—perhaps on your bathroom mirror, beside your bed, and in your office.

147

Trust the ideas that you've been Divinely receiving through repetitive and strong ideas, thoughts, and insights. The angels say, "Go for it!"

148

You have much support from the angels about the new thoughts you're putting into action. These new actions are financially successful, provided that you stay optimistic and connected to Divine guidance.

149

Your sacred mission in life is Divinely guided through inspired thoughts and ideas. Trust the messages you receive, especially as they guide you to help others.

150

Your positive thoughts and affirmations are assisting you with this change. You're fully supported by the Creator. Stay positive and optimistic, and graciously accept help as it comes to you.

151

Your thoughts are manifesting very rapidly right now, and are fueling a beneficial life change. Stay around positive-minded people, and avoid negative influences and relationships.

152

Have faith, and stay positive about the changes you're making in your life. Know that all the lessons you've learned have made you stronger and wiser.

153

The ascended masters are pushing you to make the changes you've been considering. This powerful and sacred number sequence also signifies a connection to the holy Trinity, Mother, the goddess, Mary Magdalene, and/or forgiveness.

154

Angels remind you to pay attention to your thoughts, as your expectations are creating your experiences during this time of transition and change. Call upon the angels, especially Archangel Jophiel, to help you stay positive.

155

You're experiencing a significant life change right now, and it's essential that you stay positive. Trust and know that this change is for the best.

156

All your material needs are supplied as you take the human steps necessary to commence the changes you're guided to make. Keep your thoughts positive about these changes.

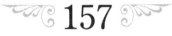

157

The Universe commends the positive changes you've made in your thoughts, beliefs, and outlook. Your optimism is well founded—keep up the good mental work!

158

Focus on positive thoughts, and consistently affirm them during this time of change. Know that the Universe supports you fully, and that this change ultimately increases your flow of abundance.

159

Hold positive thoughts and expectations about the changes you're experiencing, and know that they're preparing you for an even higher and deeper level of fulfilling your Divine life mission.

160

You access all your material needs through God and positive affirmations. Hold these feelings of gratitude and affirm that your desires have already materialized, and it is done.

161

All your material needs are supplied through your consistent and positive expectations and affirmations. Think only about what you desire, and this is what you receive.

162

Trust the guidance you're receiving about the next step to take in this situation. Your Divine guidance gives you all the information and support you need to manifest your material needs, but it requires you to really listen to your thoughts, feelings, and visions. Trust!

163

The ascended masters are assisting you with healing your thoughts about material possessions. They're showing you how to enjoy life without getting caught up in the illusion of lack or limitation.

164

Angels are ensuring that all your material needs are met. Surrender any worries you may have about material supply to the angels, and be open to receiving in miraculous ways.

165

You're changing the way in which you deal with the material world, and learning how to manifest to get your needs met. Keep holding positive thoughts and visions about your desires, and give any doubts to the Spirit world for healing and transmutation. You're a powerful manifestor!

166

You're in the perfect position to heal your life by elevating your thoughts so that they're solely focused on your heart's true desires. Let go of material concerns, and think about the beauty of Spirit. In that way, you attract beauty into your life.

167

It's important for you to acknowledge yourself for your accomplishments. Pat yourself on the back, and know that you're infinitely loved and appreciated by the Universe. Spirit is ensuring that all your material needs are supplied today and tomorrow.

168

Stay positive about material and financial issues. Your needs have always been met and will continue to be met. Positive thought, not worry, is what manifests abundance for you.

169

Take action on your Divine ideas, and see them through to completion. Let go of any fears about money, stop procrastinating or preparing, and dive into your life purpose without delay.

170

The right path for you is actualized by listening to God's Divine guidance and your own positive thoughts and visualizations. Stay focused upon God and your positive intentions.

171

You've been working hard to keep a positive outlook, and this number sequence is a sign that your commitment to manifestation work is paying off. Your intent to focus solely upon the Light is having healing effects upon others, too.

172

Your faith and optimism are well founded. You're seeing this situation clearly, and you have good reason to feel excited! Stay positive!

173

The ascended masters congratulate you on your ability to rise above negativity and to see the big picture of possibilities. Keep focused on the highest possible outcome. Well done!

174

Your angels congratulate you on your commitment to staying positive. Your optimistic outlook is an internal angel that carries you on wings of love and light, healing everyone and everything in its path.

175

Your positive intentions are helping you make this important life change right now. This change is for the best, so don't fear it. Put love into all you do.

176

Congratulations! You've found the secret to manifestation, and you're putting it into practice. Even if you can't yet see all of the results, your thoughts and prayers are on the right track. Hang in there and stay positive.

177

Your positive thoughts and affirmations have guided you to the Divine right path for you! The angels applaud your efforts. Your courage and dedication are an inspiration to others.

178

Your positive thoughts about money, abundance, and material supply are right on the mark. Visualize and affirm that you have plenty to spare and share . . . and so it is.

179

Focus your intention on the completion of this very important task. You're almost there, and this project is crucial to your Divine life mission. See it as already completed, and give thanks that it is so. It will be finished before you know it.

180

Continue to affirm your abundance to bring it into your tangible reality. Know that God wills for you to have peace concerning material supply. Turn over any fears or worries to the Creator.

181

Know that you—like everyone—deserve to receive support and prosperity. Be open to receiving, and focus only upon your desires.

182

Have faith, and know that you're financially supported now and always. You, your loved ones, and your future are safe and secure.

183

Abundance comes to you now, and one form is the flow of Divinely inspired ideas. Notice and act upon them, as they're answers to your prayers. You're financially supported as you manifest these ideas into reality.

184

The angels are helping you stay positive about money, financial flow, and material support. Call upon them both to buoy your faith, and also to manifest your needs.

185

You're going through life changes right now, which ultimately increase your flow of prosperity. It's extra important for you to stay positive, and to transform any negative beliefs about money and receiving.

186

Your positive thoughts about your life have triggered a flow of Divinely inspired ideas. Write them down and take action upon these ideas, as they bring many blessings to you and others.

187

Trust in the brilliant ideas you're receiving, as they're blueprints for manifesting everything that's important to you. Don't worry about, or procrastinate over, money issues—your supply is provided every step of the way.

188

You're manifesting a huge increase in your financial flow by holding positive thoughts, expectations, and visualizations of abundance. Stay optimistic, and follow your inner guidance.

189

Your positive thoughts, expectations, and affirmations are manifesting financial support for your Divine life mission. Keep up the good mental work!

190

You have an important life mission that's part of God's plan. Keep your thoughts peaceful, and spend time daily working on your priorities.

191

Be doubly certain that you keep your thoughts positive right now, especially related to your Divine life purpose. Stay away from addictions, and focus on creative projects. Work on your life mission without delay.

192

Have faith in the ideas and thoughts you're receiving. They're related to your life mission. Finish what you start, especially as it relates to your goals and priorities.

193

The ascended masters are with you, helping you with your life mission, organizing your schedule according to your priorities, and assisting you in staying positive. Call upon them often!

194

The angels ask you to focus upon sending light and love to the world through your natural talents and interests. The angels are with you, helping you devote time and energy to your priorities.

195

The positive changes you've made in your thoughts and beliefs are helping you manifest an even higher level for your Divine life mission. Keep your expectations optimistic!

196

It's important to take the necessary human steps on the Divine ideas you're receiving regarding your life mission. All your material needs are taken care of as you work on your goals and stay optimistic and positive.

197

You're on the right path with your plans and intentions about your Divine purpose in life. Take action today related to your priorities.

198

Dive right into your life purpose without delay or hesitation. Take Divinely guided action first, and you'll find that financial support is always there.

199

You *are* qualified and ready now for your Divine life mission. Know and feel that truth. Affirm it often.

200

Your faith has led you to a powerful and Divine connection with God. Your faith is well founded, and you're working in partnership with the Creator.

201

You're hearing your Divine guidance clearly. Have faith in yourself, stay grounded, and put this guidance into action.

202

It's important to focus on faith at this time, and to remember that you're surrounded by support from God. Your faith sets miracles into motion.

203

Your faithful connection to the ascended masters assists you in being centered in love. Keep in steady contact with the Divine, and notice, with gratitude, the miracles that occur to you and around you.

204

God and the angels ask for your patience. Stay filled with faith that your prayers have been heard and are answered.

205

Trust that the changes you're considering and experiencing are Divinely guided. Stay grounded and optimistic, and take one step at a time.

206

Your belief in God is ensuring that your material needs are always supplied. Keep the faith, and be open to receiving.

207

You're on the right path because you've trusted, and are following, Divine guidance. Keep listening and acting upon this guidance, and all will continue to be well.

208

The Creator is continuously pouring blessings upon you and your loved ones, and is providing for all of your needs. Stay centered in faith to keep this outpouring going.

209

Have faith that God and the Universe hear and support your requests about your Divine life purpose. Focus on starting and finishing one small task at a time related to your soul's desires.

210

Continue having conversations with God about your soul's desires. Keep feeling grateful for what you have and for what you're manifesting. Faith and gratitude are the magic keys for you and your manifestations.

211

Pay close attention to your thoughts about yourself and others. The more faith you have in yourself, others, and life itself, the more your faith is rewarded with positive experiences.

212

Believe in the ideas and revelations that you're receiving. Have faith in the power of your thoughts to positively alter your life.

213

Have faith in your intuition. Be open to receiving messages from ascended masters, especially the goddesses. Trust your feelings and take action accordingly.

214

The angels urge you to have faith in your ideas. Stay focused on your desires, and surrender any fears to the angels.

215

Remember how powerful your thoughts are, and keep them positive. Have faith that this change you're experiencing is manifesting your dreams and purpose.

216

Work consistently with daily affirmations to manifest your material needs and desires. Make positive statements affirming that your needs are already manifested, and have faith in the power of your intentions.

217

Your affirmations are working—keep them up! Continue to believe in the mighty manifestation power that you have, and keep focusing on your desires.

218

Faith in yourself and your higher thoughts is bringing you an abundance of prosperity. Have faith in the Divine flow of the Universe, and be open to both giving and receiving.

219

Keep positive thoughts and faith focused on your Divine life mission. Know that you're qualified and ready to help others. Use your manifestation power to create opportunities to teach and share.

220

Continue with consistent prayer, meditation, and spiritual connections with God. Open your heart fully to the Creator. Share all your feelings, hopes, and desires with God.

221

Make a mental list of everything and everyone you're grateful for. Fully feel this gratitude, and know that you'll continue to enjoy blessings throughout your life. Have faith and stay positive.

222

Have faith. Everything's going to be all right. Don't worry about anything, as this situation is resolving itself beautifully for everyone involved.

223

Call upon the ascended masters to help you stay strong and faithful. Don't fall into traps of negativity, as your faith is a necessary component to manifesting and healing right now.

224

The angels are helping you believe in yourself and your abilities. Trust in the angels, and ask for their help. Then, surrender the situation to the angels, who heal it with light and love.

225

Trust that this change is for the best. You're in a period of transition—letting go of the past and that which is no longer working. Let go, and move forward with confidence and faith.

226

Have faith that your material needs are met. Trust and follow the inner guidance that you receive, and be open to receiving help in unexpected ways.

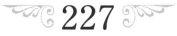

227

The angels ask you to believe in yourself and the path you've chosen, for it's the Divine right path for you!

228

You're worthy of great abundance and success, so please keep the faith. Allow yourself to receive with grace and gratitude.

229

Have faith in yourself and the guidance, ideas, and dreams you have about your Divine life mission. Even baby steps that you take today help you and others very much.

230

Have faith in the messages you receive during meditation or quiet time, as God and the ascended masters are guiding and loving you.

231

The ascended masters are helping you manifest your dreams. They ask you to keep your thoughts positively focused upon your desires, and have faith in your collective manifesting power.

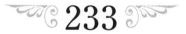

232

The ascended masters surround you and ask you to have faith. Know that they're here to support and assist you with any issue.

233

You have a strong connection with ascended masters such as Jesus. They ask you to hold faith in your mind and heart, similar to that which they demonstrated on Earth in their own lives.

234

Have faith in the angels' and ascended masters' love, and their power to miraculously assist you. Call upon them often for help, and be open to receiving their guidance and healing energy.

235

Trust in the Divine guidance you're receiving about making life changes. These are messages from the ascended masters, who know that these changes make your dreams come true. The masters support you with everything you need.

236

Have faith that the ascended masters are supplying you with everything you need in the material world. Give them any worldly concerns for healing and transmutation.

237

The ascended masters want you to know that you're on the right path. Have faith in yourself and your choices, and move forward with confidence.

238

Your connection with the ascended masters, coupled with your supreme faith, is resulting in the riches of the Universe pouring into your life. You're a living demonstration of the power of faith. Keep believing!

239

The ascended masters say, "Get to work on your life purpose now!" and ask you to have faith in your abilities to make a difference in the world. You and your mission are needed.

240

God and the angels ask you to hold faith that all is well, now and in the future. Give them any concerns or worries, and be open to receiving their help in unexpected ways.

241

Your deep faith, coupled with the angels' help and your positive thinking, are creating wondrous new miracles in your life. Stay optimistic, and continue talking with your angels about everything.

242

Your open mind and heart, as well as your belief and faith, has created a clear connection between you and your guardian angels.

243

The angels and ascended masters are with you and helping you. You can better connect with them by holding the energy of peace, faith, and trust. They ask you to believe.

244

The archangels and angels are boosting the way you see yourself so that you'll know how powerful you are. Have faith in yourself and your abilities, and trust that life is good.

245

Continue to have faith in the changes you're considering and experiencing. The angels support you during this transitional time.

246

The angels are with you, helping your material needs to be manifested. You help your prayers to be answered by staying filled with peace and faith.

247

The angels say that you're on the right path for your soul's purpose. More than ever, the angels urge you to believe in yourself and your chosen path.

248

Trust and follow the angelic messages you're receiving, as they're the answers to your prayers. As you put your Divine guidance into action, the flow of abundance increases in your life.

249

Continue to believe in your angels' guidance about your life purpose. Trust in your abilities to make the world a better place.

250

Have faith that the change you're experiencing or considering is Divinely guided and supported by God. Ask God to assist you during this transition, and be open to receiving help.

251

This transition happens easily as you continue to work with affirmations and believe them to be so. Have faith and stay positive about this life change, to ensure a smooth transition.

252

Stay filled with faith during this time of change. Be willing to release old patterns and to allow more light into your life. You are safe.

253

As you go through this life change, the ascended masters are steadying and protecting you. Give them any fears or worries, and trust in them, yourself, and your future.

254

The angels are with you during this time of change, helping you to stay filled with faith. Your optimism about the future has a powerful healing and manifesting effect.

255

Trust and have faith that this significant and important change improves your life and manifests your dreams into reality.

256

You'd like to make a life change, but worry whether you have the resources to support you. This number sequence is a message for you to surrender worries to Heaven, and to have faith in the Universe's support.

257

The Universe applauds you for taking this leap of faith. You're on the right path—keep going!

258

The changes you're considering, or are involved in, ultimately increase your flow of abundance. Stay filled with faith, trust, and optimism.

259

Keep the faith, as this change is bringing you closer to your Divine mission. Your life is becoming more settled and stable. Hang in there.

260

Trust the steps you're taking, as they're supported by God and the spirit world. Your needs are met, now and in the future.

261

See your life and your world as already healed. Trust that your needs are supplied, now and always. Avoid complaining or blaming.

262

Your prayers concerning material supply have been heard, and are answered. The more you stay centered in faith, the more you hear your Divine guidance. Trust. Everything is in Divine and perfect order.

263

The ascended masters ask you to have faith that your prayers concerning material supply have been heard and are answered. Give any worries to Jesus and the other ascended masters, and trust in their love for you and your family.

264

Your angels are with you, ensuring that your needs are met. Trust in them, and have faith in their willingness to protect and support you.

265

Your material situation and needs are changing. Have faith that you're safe and supported during this time of transition.

266

Have faith that your material needs are met, and that your world is in Divine and perfect order. The more you trust, the better the outcome.

267

You're on the right path! Your faith and affirmations ensure a steady flow of supply in your life.

268

Your manifestation work and prayers have opened the floodgates of abundance. Stay centered in faith, and be open to receiving.

269

Everything that you need to support your life mission is given to you right now, as you trust and move forward with faith.

270

God and your continued faith have put you on the right track. Trust in God's love and unlimited ability to support you in all ways.

271

Your affirmations and positive outlook have helped you find the right path. Keep up your prayers and visualizations, and trust your inner guidance about the next step to take.

272

Your faith is opening many doors for you, and will continue to do so. Trust in the way you're currently operating in life. It's working!

273

Your trust in, and relationship with, the ascended masters has created wonderful new opportunities. Walk through these doors with full faith that it's the right path for you.

274

Your angels and your faith are all illuminating the golden path you're on. This is a magical time for you. Trust and enjoy your intuition and experiences.

275

Trust that the change you're experiencing is the right thing for you. This transition ushers new love and light into your life.

276

This number sequence is a validation that you *are* on the right path, and that your material needs are sufficiently supplied. Believe in yourself, and trust that you've made the right choice.

277

You've made wise decisions by following your guidance. You're on a roll, and you can trust your intuition about the next step to take.

278

You're on the Divine right path leading to your abundance as you continue to walk in faith. Trust in, and follow, your inner guidance.

279

Your intuition and guidance about your life purpose is correct. You've completed a major chapter in your life, and it's now time to jump fully into your mission.

280

Open your arms and heart to God's infinite supply of love and abundance. God always says yes, even if the form differs from your expectations.

281

Your faith and positive affirmations ensure a steady flow of financial abundance.

282

Money is flowing to you because of your perfect faith and belief in miracles and the Divine.

283

The ascended masters ask you to trust that you'll always have enough money to abundantly care for the needs of yourself and your loved ones.

284

The angels have heard and answered your prayers concerning money. They're showering you and your loved ones with the infinite supply of the Universe. Let go of any worries.

285

Your belief in yourself is creating positive changes in your financial flow. Keep trusting and following your inner guidance.

286

Remember that your Source of abundance is within. Don't focus on external circumstances as a determiner of your abundance. They're but an illusion.

287

Continue to have faith in the path you've chosen, as it's leading you to the abundance you desire.

288

Your faith and affirmations have created waves and waves of abundance. Enjoy this blessing, and stay positive.

289

Trust that you'll always have enough money to support you in doing your life mission. Surrender any worries about financial flow, and focus solely on the giving of sacred service.

290

Trust in your ability and readiness to do God's work in the world. You are a Divine channel of healing light. Release any self-doubts to the Creator.

291

Your deep desire to help others, coupled with your faith and positive expectations, have opened new opportunities for you to manifest your Divine life mission. Listen to and follow your guidance about your path.

292

Lightworker, have faith in yourself and your mission. Release self-doubts and fears, and move confidently in the direction of your Divine guidance.

293

Surrender any procrastination tendencies toward your Divine mission to the ascended masters now. Ask them to boost your faith and confidence, and then take action on your mission without delay.

294

The angels are helping you with your life mission. Trust in the angels, and in their miraculous abilities to support you and your purpose.

295

To be fully geared toward your life mission, you first need to make some changes in your life. Trust that you already know what those changes are, and take action accordingly with full faith.

296

Trust that your material needs are supplied in order to support you in your life purpose. Your mission is important right now—don't delay it.

297

Have faith that you're on the right path with respect to your Divine mission. Any doubts only slow you down.

298

Your faith, affirmations, and the Lightwork you've been doing have tapped you in to the infinite Universal supply of abundance. You're fully supported in your life's work.

299

Get to work on your mission without delay, even if you don't yet feel prepared or qualified. Your contributions of love and light (no matter how large or small) are needed in the world—now.

300

God and the ascended masters are with you and within you right now. Your powerful connection with the highest vibrations of love and light is clear and pure. Speak with and listen to Heaven often.

301

God and the ascended masters ask you to keep your thoughts filled with love and focused upon the positive.

302

Have faith in God and the ascended masters' willingness and ability to answer your prayers. Be open to hearing their guidance and receiving their healing energy of love.

303

The ascended masters support you in your connection with God and universal wisdom, allowing you to come to a deeper understanding of your soul's purpose.

304

All of Heaven is with you, including God, the angels, and the ascended masters. Surrender any perceived problems to them, and keep your heart and mind open to their blessings of Divine love.

305

God and the ascended masters are guiding you through this Divine transition. All is well, and you are safe.

306

Allow the ascended masters and God to heal your worries. Know that God is supplying your needs.

307

God and the ascended masters applaud you for having the courage to live your truth. You are on the right path, and you are shining Divine light through your example. Stay balanced and humble.

308

Financial abundance is your Divine inheritance as a holy child of God. God and the ascended masters are showering an abundance of blessings upon you. Give to others as you feel guided.

309

God and the ascended masters are helping you with your Divine life mission. Call upon and consult with them continually about every aspect of your purpose.

310

Keep your mind and thoughts focused upon the Divine spiritual truth behind every situation and within every person. Call upon God and the ascended masters to help you stay loving and positive.

311

The ascended masters are helping—and urging—you to keep your mind focused on creating and manifesting at the highest level of light and love. Avoid addictive behaviors, as they mask your desire to create.

312

Stay positive about your future, and give any worries or concerns to the ascended masters. Your thoughts about your future have a strong influence, so focus only upon your desires, not on your fears.

313

Your strong connection with the ascended masters is helping you stay positive. They're giving you important and valid guidance about healing the world. Listen to these ideas, as they're valid.

314

The angels and ascended masters are speaking to you through Divinely inspired ideas, thoughts, and knowingness. Follow their guidance with trust and optimism.

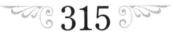

315

Your prayers, affirmations, and connection with the ascended masters has created positive change in your life. You're releasing the old and bringing in wonderful newness. Stay positive in your thoughts about yourself and your future.

316

The ascended masters ask you to hold positive thoughts about your material supply. Know that you have enough, now and always. Donate or sell that which is no longer needed.

317

You're on the right path with your work with the ascended masters. They're boosting your manifestation abilities by opening your mind to wondrous new options that are available to you.

318

Your prayers, and your connection with the ascended masters, have attracted a Divine flow of abundance. You stand in the flow of giving and receiving, which is everyone's sacred birthright.

319

Your life purpose involves working with the ascended masters. Go into quiet prayer and meditation, and talk with them about your mission. Listen for repetitive, loving messages about giving service, as this is the road map of your life.

320

The ascended masters are helping you to have perfect faith in God as an important aspect of your creative, healing, manifesting, and teaching work.

321

Your faith in the Divine has assisted you in clearly hearing the positive and loving messages of the ascended masters. They're giving you messages that help you hold loving thoughts.

322

The ascended masters ask you to believe and have faith in yourself and the spirit world. Trust in the Divine guidance you're receiving.

323

Your faith in the ascended masters is beautiful, and is an inspiration to others. Keep your faith strong and alive, as it is well founded.

324

You clearly communicate with the angels and ascended masters because of your strong faith in miracles. Trust in the messages you receive, as you're an Earth angel.

325

Your strong faith in the love of the ascended masters has brought about an important and positive change in your life. Continue to release any worries or fears about this change to the ascended masters.

326

Your prayers have been heard and answered by the ascended masters. They're ensuring that all of your needs are continuously met.

327

You've been walking in faith and following the Divine guidance you've received from the ascended masters. Because of this, you're on the right path.

328

Your faith that the ascended masters hear and answer your prayers has helped you live in the flow of Divine abundance. You're prosperous in many areas, as you stay centered in faith and keep in close contact with these Divine beings.

329

Your pure faith in, and love of, the ascended masters is helping with your Divine life purpose. Ask them any questions you may have about your mission, and trust what you receive.

330

You have a strong and clear connection with God and the ascended masters. Ask for, and be open to receiving, their help.

331

The ascended masters have gathered around you to help you stay positive, especially about the future. Ask them to help you see the good within everyone and everything (including yourself).

332

Have faith in humanity and the world's future. Remember that the ascended masters' most powerful asset is their perfect faith—be like them.

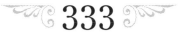

333

You've merged with the ascended masters, and they're working with you day and night—on many levels. They love, guide, and protect you in all ways.

334

The ascended masters, archangels, and angels are with you continuously, speaking with you and helping you. Ask them for help with anything. They're very real and powerful guides.

335

You're receiving Divine guidance from the ascended masters with respect to an upcoming change. Allow them to help you make it a smooth transition.

336

The ascended masters are ensuring that your material needs are met. Give any worries you have about the planet, or about material concerns, to them. Follow their guidance accordingly.

337

The ascended masters congratulate you on the path you've chosen. Please keep in close contact with them, asking them for guidance and help.

338

Your close connection with the ascended masters has helped you live the truth of their teachings: that with faith, all things are possible. Enjoy the fruits of your spiritual labor, as prosperity comes to you in many ways.

339

You're working closely with the ascended masters in your life mission. Call upon them for help and guidance with respect to your Divine life purpose.

340

You have a strong and clear connection with all of Heaven. God, the ascended masters, archangels, and angels are all with you, helping you and loving you. Call upon them often.

341

The archangels and ascended masters urge you to stay positive in your thoughts about the future. You're an Earth angel, and your optimism inspires and heals others.

342

Your faith in, and connection with, the angels and ascended masters is helping you in your spiritual healing and teaching work. You're a powerful Earth angel! Keep your faith strong by continually asking Heaven for help.

343

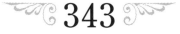

You are an Earth angel who is completely supported by the angelic realm and the ascended masters. Lean on them and be open to receiving their help in all ways.

344

You're closely connected with, deeply loved, and guided by the archangels, angels, and ascended masters. Give them any concerns or worries for healing and transmutation.

345

The angels and ascended masters are guiding and protecting you through life changes that help you in your role as an Earth angel. Surrender stress or fear about change to Heaven, for a smoother transition.

346

The angels and ascended masters want you to know that there's nothing to fear. They're ensuring that your needs are met. Give all your cares about material supply to Heaven.

347

The archangels, angels, and ascended masters say that you're on the right path. Call upon them for assistance in keeping up the good work you're doing.

348

Your work as an Earth angel, as well as your connection with the angels and ascended masters, has put you in the Divine flow of Heavenly abundance. You've learned that the Source of everything is spiritual. Now, teach this important principle to others.

349

Your purpose involves being an angel on Earth, connecting other people to their Heavenly Source for guidance and support. Ask the angels and ascended masters for specific guidance and assistance with this mission.

350

You're sheltered and protected by God and the ascended masters as you go through this much-needed life change. Surrender fears or worries about this change to Heaven, and ask for help whenever it's needed.

351

The ascended masters assist you in changing your thoughts and beliefs to a more positive and optimistic outlook. They're your source of strength while you re-create your inner world for the better.

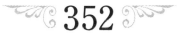

352

Have faith that the changes you're experiencing and considering bring great blessings into your life. Trust in yourself and the ascended masters to navigate through this transition with ease and harmony.

353

The ascended masters are right by your side, supporting you through all these shifts and changes. Although you may not see what's in store for you, know that this transition is for the best!

354

The angels, archangels, and ascended masters are lifting you up, helping you see the bigger picture involved with changing your life. See how these changes ultimately improve everything.

355

The ascended masters are helping, guiding, and supporting you during this time of significant change, which improves your life in new and miraculous ways.

356

You're changing your job, home, or something else in your material life. The ascended masters want you to know that they're with you every step of the way. Just ask for their help.

357

The ascended masters applaud and support this change you're embarking upon. It truly is the best choice overall.

358

The ascended masters say that the change you're making increases the flow of abundance and prosperity in many areas of your life.

359

This life change is supported by the ascended masters. You've completed your preparation, and you're now fully diving into your Divine life mission.

360

Your prayers have been heard and answered by God and the ascended masters. Give all worries, cares, and fears to Heaven, and be open to receiving help in unexpected ways.

361

You've appealed to the ascended masters for help in your prayers and affirmations. They've heard you, and are here to ensure that all of your needs are met.

362

Your faith and determination, as well as your prayers to the ascended masters, bring the healing and manifestation you've asked for. Keep affirming with faith that your prayers have already been answered.

363

The ascended masters are asking you to bring more spiritual practices into your life to balance your material focus. Examples are meditation, prayer, nature walks, reading spiritual books, and attending spiritual study groups.

364

The angels and ascended masters are helping you meet your material needs. Release and surrender your fears about this issue to them.

365

With the help of the ascended masters, you're changing the way you're looking at the material world. You're now seeing that the Source of all is spiritual. This changed consciousness attracts wonderful new opportunities.

366

The ascended masters ensure that all your material needs are met. Give them any worries, and ask them for any help you need, materially or spiritually. Be open to receiving assistance in unexpected ways.

367

You're on the right path to help the world, and to simultaneously ensure that your material needs are met while you're doing your Lightwork. The ascended masters stand by, ready to help you on your path.

368

You're putting your Divine guidance into action, and the result is an increased flow of wealth in all ways. The ascended masters are helping you, and you're listening. It's working for you!

369

Your commitment to helping the world, along with your devotion to the ascended masters, is a big part of your Divine life purpose. The ascended masters make sure that all your material needs are met while you devote yourself to your mission.

370

How beautiful you are! You're a clear channel of Divine communication, and you're putting this guidance into action. You're working in concert with God and the ascended masters to heal and help others.

371

Your positive affirmations and outlook, coupled with your prayers and meditations with the ascended masters, have led you to the right path. Keep going with these winning ways.

372

Have faith in the messages you receive from the ascended masters, as they're accurate and trustworthy. You're hearing them correctly, and you're on the right path.

373

With the team of ascended masters around you, you can't go wrong as long as you talk and listen to them frequently. You're safe, protected, and going in the right direction.

374

The archangels, angels, and ascended masters support you fully in your decisions. You're making choices based upon love and light.

375

This change that you're experiencing or considering is Divinely guided. Trust in it, and give any cares or worries about your future to the ascended masters.

376

Your connection with, and guidance from, the ascended masters has helped you release material concerns. Continue to ask Heaven for help with your earthly life, and be willing to receive Divine gifts.

377

You're on the Divine right path, as you've followed the ascended masters, who are your teachers and guides. Confidently walk the path that you're guided on.

378

You've successfully learned how to balance the material and the spiritual world, and the result is that all the riches of both worlds are bestowed upon you. Keep talking and listening to the beloved ascended masters.

379

Your thoughts, feelings, and visions about your life purpose are correct. You've been listening to Divine guidance from the ascended masters, and putting that guidance into wonderful action.

380

You've learned how to manifest consciously through your Divine connections with God and the ascended masters. Stay balanced and filled with faith by keeping in steady contact with Heaven.

381

The ascended masters ask you to raise your thoughts to a positive, new level to allow more abundance to come to you. Give any fears about money to Heaven.

382

Continue to have faith in the support and guidance you're receiving from the ascended masters about abundance. With faith, all things are possible.

383

The ascended masters surround you now to support you in all ways. They remind you that the true Source of all is Spirit, and to keep your thoughts positive to experience Heaven on Earth.

384

The angels and ascended masters are assisting you in manifesting abundance in all its rich forms.

385

The positive changes related to how you think about money—and about receiving in general—have been triggered by your prayers and connections with the ascended masters. Your new insights are attracting more prosperity into your life.

386

Balance your focus on money with prayer and spiritual practices. Give any money worries to the ascended masters, and listen with a quiet mind to their helpful guidance. The masters are ensuring that all your needs are met.

387

You've learned how to be a channel of Divine guidance, and the result is that you've stepped into the flow of universal abundance. Stick with your positive habits of prayer and meditation.

388

The ascended masters are working with you to manifest abundance for the good of all. Keep listening to and following your Divine guidance, as it's working for you.

389

The ascended masters are manifesting financial support for your life purpose. Don't delay your mission worrying about money. Help is already here.

390

God and the ascended masters are guiding and supporting your Divine life mission. Talk to them about your concerns or questions about your purpose.

391

Continue to focus on the higher thoughts of love about your life mission. Ask the ascended masters for guidance and support for your purpose.

392

Have faith in the power and guidance of the ascended masters to help you with every aspect of your Divine life mission.

393

The ascended masters are assisting you with your Divine assignment as a Lightworker. Take some time to quiet your mind through prayer and meditation in order to receive their guidance.

394

The angels and ascended masters are supporting your life mission. They ask you not to delay or procrastinate your purpose—listen as they guide you to your next step.

395

The ascended masters ask you to be open to new ways of looking at yourself and your Divine life purpose. Take quiet time to listen to their guidance about your mission.

396

You've been delaying your mission, awaiting a day when you have more time or money. The ascended masters are helping you with these issues so that you can dive into your mission without delay.

397

You're correctly hearing your Divine guidance about your life mission. The ascended masters are helping you, and you're accurately following their guidance.

398

Your life mission is very important and is fully supported by the ascended masters. Ask for, and be willing to receive, their help.

399

Your life's work is needed right now. The ascended masters ask you to give any seeming obstacles to them so that you can dive fully into your mission.

400

You have a beautiful and clear connection with God and the angels. Your heart is open to Divine love and guidance.

401

God and the angels are elevating your thoughts, belief, and consciousness to a more positive, love-based level. Give any fears or negativity to them.

402

Have faith in the power of God and the angels to help you and your loved ones in all ways.

403

All of Heaven—the Creator, ascended masters, archangels, and angels—is with you. Give all your concerns, hopes, and desires to them for healing and manifestation.

404

God and the angels surround you, your loved ones, and your current situation with powerful and healing Divine love and wisdom.

405

God and the angels guide and support you through the changes that you're considering and experiencing. These changes are part of your dreams coming true.

406

Give any concerns about material supply to God and the angels. They're with you, ensuring that all your needs are met.

407

God and the angels shine love and approval upon you and your path. They're supporting you all along the way.

408

The joyful love of God and the angels shines a light upon you, illuminating your thoughts and actions. Heaven is showering you with abundant blessings, both spiritual and material.

409

God and the angels are helping you with your Divine life mission, which they ask you to fully commit to without delay.

410

Shine the light of love upon your thoughts, and keep them positive. Give any negativity to God and the angels for healing and transmutation.

411

The angels ask you to engage in creative pursuits, and avoid addictions and negativity. You're sensitive right now, so avoid unpleasant situations and relationships. Keep your thoughts, words, and actions positive.

412

Ask the angels and archangels to come into your dreams and clear away any pessimism so that you can be filled with powerful faith and optimism.

413

The angels and ascended masters surround you and your thoughts with love and healing energy. Absorb their love into your mind so that all your thoughts shine with Divine light.

414

The angels assist you with aligning your thoughts with your highest truth. Give any worries, cares, or fears to the angels in exchange for peaceful and positive thoughts.

415

The angels ask you to give them any limiting thoughts that keep you from changing your life for the better. Be willing to improve your life, and know that the angels protect you and your future.

416

The angels heal and clear away old worries or limiting beliefs about material possessions and ownership. The angels assure you that your needs are met. Notice and receive the many gifts and blessings that come to you.

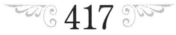

417

The angels say that your positive thoughts and optimism are well founded. You're on the right path with your intentions and actions—keep going!

418

The angels elevate your thoughts to reflect love so that you attract spiritual and material abundance.

419

The angels ask you to hold positive thoughts about your Divine life mission. You *are* qualified, ready, and able to heal and help others.

420

God and the angels remind you to stay centered in faith. Your manifestation and healing power starts with your faith and belief. Give doubts to Heaven.

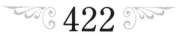

421

The angels ask you to use positive affirmations to buoy your faith, such as, "I have perfect faith right now."

422

The angels urge you to have faith, and trust in them and in yourself. See the angel within you and other people to help you believe in the good of humanity.

423

The archangels and ascended masters ask you to believe in them . . . and in yourself. You have powerful helpers by and on your side.

424

You're surrounded by the help and powerful healing love of angels. Stay centered in faith and belief, as this allows the angels to help you even more.

425

The angels ask you to have faith that the changes you're experiencing and considering are for the best. Everything is okay in truth.

426

Your prayers, faith, and connection with the angels ensure that your needs are met. Keep believing, and give any worries to the angels.

427

The angels say that you're on the right path, and have good reason for optimism. Your faith in the Divine guidance you're receiving from the angels is a big reason for your success.

428

Your faith-filled prayers and affirmations have been heard and answered. The angels ensure that you have a steady flow of abundance in all ways.

429

Your beautiful faith in the angels opens doors of opportunity for you and your Divine life mission. Step through those doors with confidence.

430

God, the angels, ascended masters, and the entire Universe support you completely! Ask Heaven for help with any matter.

431

The angels and ascended masters ask you to stay positive about yourself, your life, and your future. Give any fears or worries to Heaven for healing and transmutation.

432

Have faith in the repetitive messages you're receiving from the angels and ascended masters. This is real and trustworthy guidance.

433

You're loved, guided, and supported by the angels and ascended masters. Keep Heaven and spirituality foremost in your thoughts.

434

Your prayers have been heard and answered by the many angels and ascended masters who are at your side right now. Continue talking with them about everything, and notice the many miracles they bring you.

435

The angels and ascended masters make your life changes smooth and harmonious. Ask them to help you with the small and large aspects of this change.

436

The angels and ascended masters help all your needs to be met. You and your future are safe and protected.

437

The angels and ascended masters congratulate you on the path you've chosen. Keep up the good work!

438

Heaven is helping you with your finances. Give any money worries to the angels and ascended masters, and follow their Divine guidance to manifest abundance.

439

Your Divine life purpose is fully supported by the angels and ascended masters. Talk to them about any questions or concerns about your mission.

440

You're deeply loved by God and the angels. They're with you, helping you, now and always. Call upon them for help and healing.

441

The angels are with you, helping you keep your thoughts positive and loving. Call upon them for help in *staying* positive.

442

Your faith and prayers have attracted many angels to your side. They love you, and ask you to keep believing in the power of miracles. Your faith creates and attracts them!

443

Your faith and prayers have attracted many
The archangels, angels, and ascended masters are with you right now, helping you with this situation and anything else you need. Call upon them, and be open to their help and guidance.

444

Thousands of angels surround you at this moment, loving and supporting you. You have a very strong and clear connection with the angelic realm, and are an Earth angel yourself. You have nothing to fear—all is well.

445

The angels are guiding you through an important life change. Please allow them to help make the transition smooth.

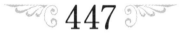

446

Your prayers about getting your needs met have attracted the help of many angels. Give them any worries or questions you may have, and be open to receiving their assistance.

447

You're working with the angels to help make the world a better place. The angels are grateful for your partnership and ask you to keep up the great work.

448

The "Angels of Abundance" are with you, helping you to receive your Divine inheritance.

449

Your life purpose involves sharing your knowledge of the angels with others. The angelic realm is helping you with this, as well as additional aspects of your mission.

450

God and the angels help you through the change you're experiencing or considering. Work as a team with Heaven by giving them your cares, asking for help, and being open to receiving Divine help.

451

The angels ask you to hold a positive mind-set about making life changes. Your optimism, coupled with the angels' help, makes the transition much smoother.

452

Have faith that the angels are helping you change your life for the better. To bring in the new, you must release the past.

453

The angels and ascended masters urge you to make necessary life changes *now*. Put these changes front-and-center on your schedule, and know that Heaven is helping you along the way.

454

The angels tell you to focus on the good during this time of change. They remind you that courage is the willingness to depart from the familiar.

455

The angels guide and support you through a significant and much-needed life change. Trust and follow their guidance.

456

The angels applaud the actions you're taking to improve your life. Give any cares or worries to the angels, as they wish to help you.

457

Your recent change in direction has helped put you more squarely on the right path. The angels applaud and support you.

458

The angels say that the more steps you take to improve yourself and your life, the more you open the floodgates of Divine abundance.

459

The angels help you remove obstacles to your life purpose. Call on them to get specific guidance and help.

460

Give all your cares and worries about getting your needs met to God and the angels. Let go of fears about your future, as they can block you from hearing Divine guidance.

461

The angels ask you to maintain a positive outlook about your needs being met and about your future. Your optimism opens the channels of angelic assistance.

462

Have faith that the angels have heard, and answered, your prayers. Your needs are met, now and always.

463

Don't struggle alone with worries and fears! Give them to the angels and ascended masters, who are with you right now and who wish to help you with everything.

464

The angels assist you with the human steps to take in this situation. Move forward in trust.

465

With the help of the angels, you're undergoing a significant change that increases your flow of material supply. Talk to Heaven, and listen to the angels' messages.

466

Your angels want you to give them all your cares, worries, and concerns. Work as a team with Heaven to approach any seeming problem.

467

You're on the right path, and the angels ask you to stop worrying, as everything is on track.

468

Don't worry about money. The angels guide you to financial freedom, as you ask for their help and are then open to hearing and receiving their guidance.

469

Give the angels any concerns or confusion you have about your Divine life purpose. They're here to give you clarity and courage about your mission.

470

God and the angels support and applaud the path you're on. Keep up the good work!

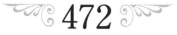

471

The angels say that you're on the right path to elevate your thoughts and consciousness to a very powerful level. The angels help you become even more powerful and dynamic by asking you to focus on love and light.

472

The angels applaud you and ask you to continue to have faith in your path. You're on the right course.

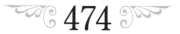

473

The angels and ascended masters acknowledge your wonderful progress on this path. Keep going!

474

The angels surround you, and they support your intentions and great work. Angels illuminate your every footstep—you can't fail.

475

The shifts you're experiencing are what you've prayed for in order to align with your Divine path and the angels.

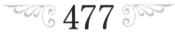

476

The angels say that you're on the right path, and not to worry. Your needs are met, now and in the future.

477

Your connection with the angelic realm has led you to the Divine right path! The angels applaud your courage and commitment to the Light.

478

You're on the path of Divine abundance. Continue to allow the angels to guide you.

479

The angels bless you and the path of your Divine purpose. They congratulate you for following your guidance.

480

Allow God and the angels to connect with you during quiet meditation in order to assist you with abundance issues.

481

You've got the right outlook to attract abundance into your life. The angels say that your positive intentions help and inspire others, too.

482

Continue to have faith in the messages you're receiving from the angels about abundance. This guidance helps you manifest all your needs.

483

The angels and ascended masters assist you with manifestation. Pay close attention to the messages that come to you in the form of repetitive thoughts, ideas, feelings, and visions. These are answers to your prayers.

484

The angels surround you and your finances with Divine love. By giving your cares to the angels and listening to their Divine guidance, your abundance is assured.

485

The angels assist you in making a positive change in your financial life. Be open to their help and healing.

486

The angels ask you to give them your insecurities about money, especially those relating to your financial future. Let go of any "bag lady" or "homeless man" worries. You've always been provided for, and you always will be.

487

The angels acknowledge you and the path you've chosen to attain your abundance.

488

The angels guide you to your abundance. Release any fears, and allow this abundance to flow to you easily and comfortably.

489

The angels bring you the material and financial support you need for your Divine life purpose. Don't procrastinate your mission, awaiting more money. The time is now.

490

God and the angels fully support your beautiful life purpose. Make your mission your top priority, and listen for Divine guidance as to the next steps to take.

491

The angels ask you to stay optimistic and think positive thoughts about fulfilling your Divine life purpose. Remember that you're a holy child of God in all ways, which means that you're completely qualified and prepared for your mission.

492

Have faith in the angels' willingness and ability to help you with every aspect of your Divine purpose. Just ask them for help, and then be willing to receive their blessings and miracles.

493

The angels and ascended masters are with you as you fulfill your life purpose. They say that your mission is much needed in the world, and they wish to help you with it.

494

The angels are fully supportive of your Divine mission. They tell you the details of your purpose through your repetitive thoughts, feelings, and visions. Listen closely.

495

You're guided by the angels to make the necessary changes that give you more time and energy to devote to your Divine life mission. Ask the angels to help you with every aspect of these changes and your purpose.

496

The angels ask you to make your Divine life mission your top priority right now. Don't worry about how it will come about, or any other material aspect concerning your purpose. The angels help with everything.

497

The angels confirm that you're on the right path for your Divine mission in life. Even if you can't see exactly where you're headed, the angels can, and they say that it's beautiful and healthy.

498

Your focus upon, and commitment to, your Divine purpose, is fully supported by the angels. The angelic realm supports your mission spiritually and materially.

499

The angels say, "Get to work on your life mission now, without delay! Your purpose is much needed in the world." If you're unsure of what your purpose is, or what steps to take toward it, call upon and listen to the angels.

500

God and the Universe support the changes you're making. They emphasize that these changes are essential, and that it's safe for you to make them.

501

During this time of transformational change, stay connected to God through prayer and positive affirmations. Surrender any fears or needs to the Creator, especially while going through these changes.

502

Your faith in God supports you during this time of change. Remember to take quiet time and do things to nurture yourself.

503

God and the ascended masters support the changes you're experiencing or considering. They're guiding and protecting you every step of the way.

504

This time of transition moves quickly and easily as you allow the angels and God to support you.

505

Put God at the center of all your thoughts, and your life changes for the better very quickly.

506

Keep your thoughts focused upon Spirit during this time of change, and the material will take care of itself.

507

The changes that you're Divinely guided to undertake are a good idea. They put you on the right path.

508

God Divinely guides and supports the changes that you're experiencing, and ensures a steady flow of financial support.

509

God assists you in making important life changes that help your overall Divine life purpose. Spend quiet time in prayer and meditation, and take action upon the guidance you receive.

510

Hold positive thoughts about the changes that you're Divinely guided to make. Your optimism helps this transition be smooth and harmonious.

511

You're going through positive changes in the way you think and look at the world. Stay away from addictions, and engage in creative pursuits. Use positive affirmations daily.

512

Your positive thoughts and faith are ushering in remarkable changes in yourself and your life. Enjoy the transformations you're instigating with your powerful intentions.

513

Your prayers and connections with the ascended masters, especially the goddesses, are changing your life for the better.

514

The angels are with you, helping you stay centered and peaceful during this time of change. Rest assured that your life is transforming in a beautiful way.

515

You have the power to change your life in amazing ways, simply by changing your thoughts and beliefs. Now more than ever, it's important to only focus upon what you desire.

516

Your positive affirmations are elevating your beliefs and thoughts, ensuring that you'll always have plenty of everything you need.

517

The positive changes you're making in your thoughts and actions have put you on the right course. Keep up the good work!

518

Now that you're looking at yourself in a much more positive way, you realize that it's okay for you to receive an abundance of good. Congratulations on honoring yourself in this way!

519

You're now realizing how powerful you are and the importance of your Divine life mission. Adopting a more positive self-concept is helping you with your purpose.

520

Have faith in God to help you change your life for the better. Miracles can rapidly transform situations, so expect them to occur!

521

Keep elevating your faith so that you expect only the best out of people and life. Your positive expectations create wonderful new experiences and opportunities.

522

Keep the faith, and change any pessimistic viewpoints to ones of optimism. As you believe, so it is done to you.

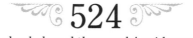

523

Have confidence in the ascended masters' abilities to help you change your life for the better. Trust in their power and love, and give them any fears or worries.

524

You've clearly heard the angels' guidance about making necessary changes. Trust in this Divine guidance, and follow it without delay.

525

Trust, believe, and have faith that the changes you're making are for the best. Everyone benefits from these transformations.

526

Have faith that your daily needs are met, now and in the future. Let go of worries, and focus upon your heart's desires instead.

527

Trust that the changes you're making are the right ones, and that they put you on the correct path.

528

Now that your faith level is higher, your flow of abundance is higher as well. Keep going, and increase your levels of faith and abundance even more.

529

Have faith that the changes you're making are important for your overall Divine purpose.

530

Your connection with the ascended masters is helping you know God on a deeper level. Beautiful!

531

The ascended masters are helping you change your thoughts to a more positive viewpoint. This, in turn, changes your life in wonderful and miraculous ways.

532

Have faith that the ascended masters are fully supporting you through the changes you're considering or are making.

533

The ascended masters support this Heaven-guided change. Remember that you're a Divine alchemist, and this transition can be all that you wish.

534

The ascended masters and angels encourage you to make these much-needed changes. Give them any cares, questions, or worries.

535

The ascended masters are at the "eye of the hurricane" during this whirlwind time of change for you. They assist you with every detail, including helping you to stay centered and peaceful.

536

The ascended masters say that this change increases the flow of guidance and support you receive. Heaven is ensuring that your needs are supplied, especially during this transition time. Let go!

537

The ascended masters congratulate you on the changes you're making, as they're putting you squarely on the right path.

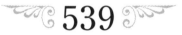

538

The ascended masters help you make the necessary changes to increase the flow of your abundance.

539

Instead of trying to understand and work on your purpose singlehandedly, you're now working as a team with the ascended masters . . . and it's working for you and your purpose!

540

There's a wonderful change coming your way, which is needed and supported by God and the angels.

541

As you go through this change, keep in constant contact with your angels to help you stay optimistic. Your positive thoughts, coupled with the angels' help, ensure a smooth and happy transition.

542

Have faith in the power and love of your guardian angels during this time of change. Call upon the angels often.

543

The angels and ascended masters guide you through these important life changes. Lean on them for support and assistance.

544

The angels and archangels urge you to make an important life change your top priority (you already know what it is). Call upon the angels to motivate and support you during this time.

545

You're going through major transitions in nearly every life area. The angels say that these changes bring more light, love, and blessings into your life, and they're helping you every step of the way.

546

The angels help you manifest, and let go of, the old ways of struggling to meet your needs. Get in touch with the power that you and the angels have, and use it with clear intentions to manifest your desires.

547

You're on the right path with respect to the changes you're making or considering. The angels are with you every step of the way.

548

The angels are altering your relationship with money. You're realizing that Spirit is your Source for everything you need in this life. This realization is making you more confident and relaxed.

549

The angels are shifting you energetically to prepare you for the next step in your Divine life purpose. Be open to the angels' guidance about making changes to your lifestyle, such as eating, reading, communing with nature, and so on.

550

The major changes that you're experiencing are Divinely guided. God is helping you through this time of change with love, light, and blessings.

551

Your positive thoughts, affirmations, and intentions have created a big change in your life, which improves your life significantly.

552

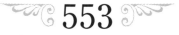

Have faith in the choices you've made about changing your life. Life is becoming more stable and calm. In the meantime, trust in the movement that's positively altering your life.

553

The ascended masters support the changes you're experiencing or considering. Ask them for help before and during this transition.

554

You're changing several aspects of your life simultaneously. The angels are next to you, supporting and guiding you through this transition.

555

Major changes and significant transformations are here for you. You have an opportunity to break out of the chrysalis and uncover the amazing life you truly deserve.

556

The changes you're experiencing help you with material and earthly desires. Keep your sacral chakra (near the base of your spine) clear and balanced to continue bringing these desires into your reality.

557

Your path has been one of significant change, and Heaven applauds the courage and tenacity you've displayed. You've wisely chosen to walk through these changes!

558

The flow of abundance is plentiful as you move through this transition. Keep releasing your past patterns to Spirit.

559

A major change is helping you with your life purpose. You're also a teacher of change on all levels and aspects. Please step forward and share your wisdom.

560

Your prayers, and open-hearted connection with the Divine, help you release old fears and worries about material supply. You're now open to receiving the blessings that Heaven bestows upon you. Stay immersed in gratitude, and release your worries to God.

561

Your new, more positive outlook about your material supply is working for you. Notice all the gifts that come your way, and pass them along as you feel guided. Your gratitude keeps the flow going.

562

Your newfound faith and renewed commitment to visualization and manifestation is bringing new opportunities and material supply to you. Keep the faith!

563

The positive change that you've undergone has transformed you into a powerful manifestor. With your spiritual power and the help of the ascended masters, all your material needs are infinitely supplied.

564

Now that you've called upon the angels for help with your material supply, your needs are met in miraculous ways. Keep working with the angels to manifest your needs.

565

You've radically improved the way in which you view the material world. You're learning how to manifest, instead of struggle, to get your needs met.

566

Fears and worry can block your flow of material supply. Release these concerns to Heaven. Ask for help, without specifying exactly how that help will appear. Be open to receiving the good that comes to you.

567

You're now seeing the material world, and the way to access supply, correctly. Your new plan of action has put you on the right path. Congratulations!

568

You're beginning to manifest more money, thanks to the recent changes you've made in learning how to create what you want through right action.

569

A change in the way you view material resources and supplies is helping you manifest your Divine life purpose. Take action on your mission first and your material needs are supplied.

570

The change you're experiencing is aligning you with your Divine right path. Allow God to support you, and know that you're not alone.

571

The positive changes you've made in your thoughts and affirmations have put you on the right path.

572

You're on the right path with the changes you're making. Keep the faith.

573

Well done! You've been listening to, and accepting guidance from, the ascended masters. With their help, you're now on the right path.

574

The angels are helping you change your life for the better. Keep asking the angels for assistance, and then follow their guidance. It's working for you!

575

The huge changes that you're experiencing and considering bring great blessings to you and your loved ones. Keep going!

576

Your changed outlook on manifesting material supply is working. You've learned how to manifest your needs into reality.

577

You've gone through a wonderful transformation, and all your work and dedication has paid off. Congratulations!

578

You're on the right path to increasing your flow of abundance through the changes you're making.

579

The recent changes you've been making have put you on the right path for your Divine life mission.

580

God is with you during this time of change and helps you increase your level of abundance.

581

By changing your thoughts about money, you've opened the floodgates of abundance. Keep up the positive thoughts and affirmations, as they're working!

582

Have faith in the changes you're making, as they're bringing you abundance in all ways. Keep your heart filled with gratitude, and release all worries to Heaven.

583

The changes you're making are guided by the ascended masters. They're helping you manifest all the abundance you need, with plenty to spare and share.

584

The angels are with you, helping you make important life changes. Your flow of abundance is changing for the better, thanks to your work with the angels.

585

Your financial situation is markedly improving. Expect an increased flow of abundance.

586

The changes you're making improve your financial situation and help you meet all your (and your loved ones') needs.

587

You're on the right path to shifting and increasing the flow of your abundance.

588

The change you're considering assists you in claiming your abundance. Release any fears, and allow your abundance to flow to you easily and comfortably.

589

You're now fully committing to your Divine life purpose, and your commitment has increased your flow of abundance. Your purpose is supported in all ways.

590

God asks you to change your life to fully commit to your Divine life purpose. Put love at the core of everything, without delay, and give any cares to God for healing.

591

Stay positive about your Divine mission. Your life is changing to allow you more time for, and clarity about, your purpose.

592

Have faith that the changes you're making support your Divine mission.

593

The ascended masters urge you to make the necessary changes to commit to your life mission. You and your purpose are very important, so focus upon it without fear or delay.

594

Your angels support your Divine mission. They're healing your life to allow you more time, energy, and other resources to devote to your purpose.

595

Focus solely on giving spiritual service to the world, which is your Divine mission, and your life automatically changes and heals for the better.

596

Everything you need for your Divine mission is supplied to you. It's safe for you to change your life and fully devote yourself to your purpose.

597

Your new commitment and devotion to your Divine purpose has put you on the right path in all areas of your life. Keep going!

598

Now that your Divine mission is at the core of your thoughts and actions, you've opened the floodgates of abundance. Stay focused and devoted, and know that there's nothing to fear.

599

Make your Divine life purpose your top priority. Change or heal anything that's blocking you, as your mission is very important and needed right now.

600

God and the Universe supply all your needs. Give any cares or worries about your material supply to the Creator, and be open to receiving miracles and blessings.

601

Pray and affirm that God meets all your needs, and it is done.

602

Have faith in God's loving power to heal and supply everything you need. Ask the Creator for help, and expect miracles!

603

God and the ascended masters help you receive everything you and your loved ones need.

604

The Creator and the angels have heard, and answered, your prayers. Be open to receiving in wonderfully surprising ways.

605

God is helping you change your work life so that your spiritual and physical needs are always met.

606

Allow God to be the center of your support so that all third-dimensional needs flow easily to you and your loved ones.

607

God blesses the path you're on, and meets all your material needs.

608

Give all money worries to God, and be open to receiving all the blessings and abundance that are coming to you in mysterious and miraculous ways.

609

God helps you manifest everything you need for your Divine life mission. Let go, and let God help you completely.

610

Your positive thoughts and affirmations co-create an infinite of supply of good for you and your loved ones.

611

It's essential for you to keep your thoughts about your material supply focused upon your desires, not your fears.

612

Have faith that your prayers, affirmations, and visualizations are manifesting with Divine timing and in perfect order. The more you walk in faith, the more you experience the flow of supply coming to you.

613

Your prayers to the ascended masters have been heard and answered. They're ensuring that all your needs are met.

614

The angels ask that you stay positive as you work with them to manifest your desires into reality. You and the angels are a team.

615

Your new positive attitude and the affirmations you've adopted help you manifest everything you need.

616

Keep your thoughts positive, expect miracles, and know that your needs are met. Give any fears to Heaven for healing, as worries block your manifestations. Stay optimistic, and know that everything is in Divine and perfect order.

617

Through your positive affirmations, you're on the right path to manifesting everything you need. Keep up the positive thoughts, as they're working!

618

Know that God is your Divine Source for abundance, and give any money worries to Heaven for healing and transmutation. Your spiritual understanding of money has put you into the Divine flow of abundance.

619

Don't delay your life purpose because of concerns about money or material needs. Instead, use your God-given power of manifestation to visualize all your needs into existence.

620

Trust that God is supporting your material needs, as well as those of this world. The more you believe, the more you notice God's blessings and miracles.

621

Your continued belief and work with affirmations ensures that your needs are met in miraculous ways.

622

Faith is the key to manifesting everything you need. The more faith you hold, the more miracles you notice and experience.

623

The ascended masters ensure that your material needs are met. They ask you to stay peacefully centered in the knowledge that all is well.

624

Your faith in the angels' love and power has allowed them to help you, materially and spiritually. Keep believing in the angels and in miracles!

625

Your faith and belief are creating positive changes, which help you and your loved ones enjoy a better life. There's truly nothing to fear or worry about.

626

The answer to your prayers is your amazing power of faith and belief. Rise above all illusions of problems, and claim the spiritual truth that everything is in Divine order. Your faith brings about miracles.

627

Your faith is warranted and well founded, as it's helping to ensure that all your needs are met.

628

Believe more in miracles than in the illusion of problems, especially where money is concerned. Invest in positive thinking, and you'll reap dividends very quickly.

629

Keep believing that your Divine purpose financially supports you. Your faith in this principle makes it a reality.

630

God and the ascended masters watch over you and your loved ones, ensuring that you're well taken care of. With such powerful help, you needn't worry.

631

Keep asking the ascended masters for guidance about the next step for you to take, and then walk in confidence as you follow this guidance. Give any material concerns to the ascended masters.

632

The ascended masters ask you to stay optimistic and faith-filled concerning your material needs being met. They're guiding you in all ways; just listen to and follow them.

633

Many ascended masters surround you and offer an infinite supply of help. They're protecting, guiding, and providing for you and your loved ones.

634

Have no worries—the angels and ascended masters are with you, ensuring that your material needs are supplied, now and always.

635

The ascended masters help you change your beliefs so that you're no longer caught up in the illusion of scarcity and lack. Your new abundant thinking helps you manifest all your needs quickly and easily.

636

Give all your cares or worries about material concerns to the ascended masters, who love you and want to meet your needs.

637

The ascended masters congratulate the work you've been doing, as it has put you on the right path to ensure a steady flow of material support and supply.

638

The ascended masters assure you that you'll always have enough money. They ask you to let go of worrying about finances, and to allow them to guide and help you.

639

The ascended masters support your Divine life purpose materially and spiritually. Let go of worrying, and focus upon your mission.

640

Give any material concerns to God and the angels, who are with you right now, helping you in all ways.

641

The angels assist with your manifesting by helping you see your desires as already being a reality. Work with these Heavenly beings to stay positively centered in the magnetic energy of gratitude.

642

The angels ask you to keep the faith that all your needs are supplied, as they're helping you with this manifestation. Give any worries to Heaven for healing and transmutation.

643

The angels and ascended masters watch over you and your family to ensure that all your needs are met. Release stress to Heaven.

644

The archangels, along with the rest of the angelic realm, assist you with all earthly and material issues.

645

Be open to changes, as they bring you the answers to your prayers. The angels enhance your life by helping you let go of that which is out of balance or unneeded.

646

Give every one of your cares, worries, and fears to the angels. Know that they're with you always, helping you with everything.

647

The steps you're taking are in perfect alignment with the guidance from your angels.

648

The angels help you replace lack and scarcity with abundance and prosperity. First, this occurs in your thoughts and beliefs, and then in the material world.

649

Now is the time to work on your Divine life mission, as the archangels and angels fully support you in all ways.

650

This current transformation helps you break free of material limitations. Trust the steps you're guided to take, and allow God to support you.

651

Take some contemplation time through meditation to be crystal clear about your soul's desires. Hold positive thoughts about making any necessary changes, and give any worries to Heaven for healing.

652

Have faith that the changes you're experiencing or considering help you to manifest materially.

653

The ascended masters guide you to make significant and important changes, which better ensure that your material needs are met.

654

The changes you're considering regarding your behavior, habits, or patterns are supported by the angels.

655

You're experiencing significant change, which ultimately brings beautiful blessings into your world. Be open to this change, as it's definitely for the best.

656

You're changing the way in which you view the material world so that you easily meet your material needs, instead of struggling.

657

The steps you're taking put you on the right path, resulting in your desired transformation. All your needs are met along the way.

658

This change is creating a positive influence on your finances. Let go of material concerns, and focus on following your Divine guidance.

659

You're committed to your Divine life purpose, and are willing to take the human steps necessary to enact your mission. Stay open-minded, flexible, and positive.

660

Balance your focus on the material with time spent in spiritual contemplation. God helps you meet your needs. Give any worries or stress to Heaven for healing and transmutation.

661

Your thoughts create your experience. Act as if your desires have already manifested, because they have in spiritual truth.

662

Have faith that your material needs are supplied, and take human steps to put your Divinely guided ideas into action.

663

The ascended masters help you take action on your Divine guidance to ensure that all your needs are met.

664

Give any stress or material concerns to the angels. They're with you, and are ensuring that your needs are infinitely supplied.

665

Material and earthly matters are resolved as you make Divinely guided changes. Listen to your gut feelings and intuition, as they're guiding you on how to find answers to your prayers.

666

It's time to focus on Spirit to balance and heal your life. Tell Heaven about any fears you have concerning material supply. Be open to receiving help and love from both humans and the angels.

667

You're on the right path to transmute material illusions of scarcity and competition into infinite supply. Keep up your spiritual practices of prayer and meditation to achieve balance.

668

You're now entering a wonderful new time where your financial needs are supplied through Divine love, and not from fears of scarcity. Stay focused on Spirit, the true Source of your supply.

669

Let go of any material concerns related to your Divine life purpose, and know that you're presently qualified to fulfill your important mission.

670

Your prayers about material issues have been heard and are answered by God. Have no fear or worries.

671

Your positive affirmations and visualizations are working, and are helping you manifest your needs. Keep going!

672

Have faith that earthly, material desires are coming to you as you take your Divinely guided steps.

673

Your prayers and connections with the ascended masters help you in all ways, including ensuring that your material needs are amply met.

674

The angels support the steps you're taking in this matter, and they want you to know that you're on the right track. Give any worries to the angels, and allow them to help you with earthly issues.

675

You've made (and are making) some changes that have put you on the right path to manifesting an increased material supply.

676

You're on the right path to manifesting an infinite supply of earthly necessities. Give any material concerns to Heaven, and follow your Divine guidance fearlessly.

677

You're taking the human steps to put your Divine guidance into action. All your needs are supplied along the way. Keep up the good work!

678

The action that you're taking has put you on the right path to abundance. Give any cares or worries to Heaven.

679

It's best to give your Divine life purpose your full attention right now. Don't worry about material concerns, as they're taken care of. Just focus on your mission.

680

There's nothing to worry about. God is meeting your material and financial needs. Continue deepening your connection to Heaven through prayer and meditation.

681

Keep your thoughts about money and manifestation positive, and give all your worries to Heaven for transmutation and healing. Your affirmative thoughts are manifesting the abundance you desire.

682

Have faith in the steps you're taking, as they lead to Divine abundance.

683

Nitze The ascended masters help you release fears concerning money, and encourage you to be open to receiving abundance in Divinely guided ways.

684

The angels ensure that your material needs are abundantly met and that you're financially secure.

685

You've made positive changes in the way you think about and act toward money. Give any remaining fears about your finances to Heaven, and allow abundance to come your way.

686

You're letting go of the old pattern of feast or famine, and learning how to manifest financial security and consistency of income. Keep releasing money fears to Heaven, and trust in your Divine guidance.

687

You're on the right path with the actions you've taken in this matter to manifest Divine abundance in all ways.

 688

As you let go of material concerns, you've opened the way for waves of abundance to come to you. Keep trusting in Heaven to support you and meet your needs.

689

Put your focus solely on "How may I serve?" and don't even think about money. Your life purpose ensures that all of your material needs are met now and in the future.

690

God is Divinely guiding you to help others, and is supplying everything you need for the fruition of your life mission.

691

Your positive intentions, thoughts, and affirmations have opened the way for your Divine purpose to be fully supported by Heaven. Don't worry about a thing; just focus on your mission.

692

Have faith that all your needs are met as you work on your Divine life mission.

693

The ascended masters supply your material needs while you focus on your Divine purpose in life. Ask them to help you with all aspects of your mission.

694

The angels are with you, guiding every step of your soul's purpose. Focus upon service, and allow the angels to support you in all ways.

695

The changes that you've made have enabled you to focus on your Divine life purpose. All your needs are met as you take steps to enact your mission.

696

Let go of any material concerns that could delay your mission. Your Divine life purpose is very important and much needed right now. Focus on your purpose, and all your needs are supplied.

697

You're on the right path with your Divine mission. Continue to co-create the manifestation of all your needs through prayer and affirmation, and by following your inner guidance.

698

As you let go of fears and procrastination tendencies, the doors of your Divine life purpose open widely. Focus on giving service and following your soul's passion—everything else will take care of itself.

699

Get to work, Lightworker! Don't delay your mission because of material concerns. Instead, concentrate on helping the world through your inner guidance and passions. All your needs are met as you focus on service.

700

God and the Universe congratulate you on the wonderful path you're on. Keep up the good work!

701

Your positive thoughts, affirmations, and prayers have put you on the right path. God is watching over you and helping you all along the way.

702

Your faith in God's loving, healing, and providing power has placed you on the right course. Keep listening to and following God's Divine wisdom.

703

Your heart-centered connections with God and the ascended masters have given you trustworthy guidance, which you're following with miraculous results.

704

You're listening to, and following, Divine guidance from God and the angels. They're helping you with every aspect of your life.

705

The change that you've been Divinely guided to make has placed you on the right path. God is helping and watching over you during this change—and always.

706

You're hearing God's guidance correctly, and by following it, you're helping to answer your prayers.

707

You're working in perfect union with God the Creator. Your willingness to trust, listen, surrender, and follow brings great miracles into your life.

708

God is telling you that you're on the right path and are reaping a great bounty of abundance.

709

You've been listening to God's guidance about your life purpose with great accuracy. Trust and follow your intuition.

710

Your positive thoughts and prayers have brought much joy and manifestation into your life. Stay grateful, positive, and connected to God through prayer and meditation.

711

Congratulations! You've really devoted yourself to positive affirmations and visualizations, and you're starting to see the miraculous results. Keep going.

712

Your faith and positive affirmations have put you on the right path. You're on a roll, and miracles abound. Keep up the good work!

713

The ascended masters are with you, and your positive intentions and thoughts have opened the door for them to help you to heal and manifest. Stay positive and connected.

714

The angels congratulate you on your positive thoughts and affirmations. They lead you along the right course of action, and Heaven helps you every step of the way.

715

The Divinely inspired change that you're considering or experiencing brings you countless blessings.

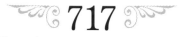

716

You're changing your beliefs about getting your needs met. Instead of struggling for your good, you're learning to manifest . . . and you're doing it well!

717

Your affirmations, prayers, and visualizations are wonderfully inspired and are bringing you the answers to your prayers. Keep up the good mental and spiritual work!

718

Your positive affirmations about finances have opened up the floodgates of abundance for you. Stay positive and connected with Spirit about this issue.

719

You're on the right path in the way that you're thinking about, planning, and taking action on your life purpose. You're hearing your Divine guidance accurately and correctly.

720

Your faith in God has helped you to hear and trust your Divine guidance. You're following that guidance and are embarking on a beautiful path illuminated with God's love and protection.

721

Continue deepening your faith and saying positive affirmations, as you're experiencing miraculously beautiful results.

722

Your deep convictions have placed you firmly on the right path. Keep the faith!

723

You're walking in faith, based upon the guidance given to you by the ascended masters. You're on the right course; and you're protected, loved, and watched over.

724

You've kept the faith and have followed your Divine guidance. The angels applaud your work.

725

Remember to keep believing in the changes you've made, as you *are* doing the right thing.

726

Your actions of faith have put you on the right track to receiving all the answers to your prayers.

727

The Spirit world applauds your total and complete faith. Your willingness to listen to, and trust in, Heaven has put you on the right path.

728

Continue on this path, as it's bringing you the abundance you desire. Be willing to receive guidance and all the gifts Heaven offers you.

729

Continue to have faith in your ability to fulfill your Divine life purpose. You correctly understand enough about your mission to put it into action.

730

God and the ascended masters are with you, and you're hearing their guidance correctly. Allow them to help you in all ways.

731

The ascended masters applaud your positive affirmations, intentions, and efforts. Even if you can't see the results yet, keep going. The masters say that you're on the right path.

732

Continue to have faith in the path you've chosen, as it brings forth a closer connection to Divine truth, as well as the miracles manifested through the ascended masters.

733

The ascended masters support your path and ask you to continue the great work. They're with you continuously, listening to your prayers and guiding your steps.

734

The angels and ascended masters send you kudos about the direction you've chosen. They surround you and your path with love, light, and great blessings.

735

Your decision to make changes is fully supported by the ascended masters. You've made the right choice, and they want to help you with this transition.

736

You're on the right path, and the ascended masters take care of you and your loved ones. They ensure that all your needs are met. No worries!

737

You're clearly and accurately hearing the Divine wisdom of the ascended masters. Your willingness to follow their guidance has put you on the right path.

738

Your work with the ascended masters has helped you manifest new abundance. Keep walking on the path of your Divine guidance, and open your arms to receive great blessings and miracles.

739

You're on the right path, and are working with the ascended masters on your Divine life purpose. Keep calling upon Heaven for help, and trust the loving guidance that's given to you.

740

You're clearly and correctly hearing the Divine infinite wisdom of God and the angels. They're with you, helping you put this guidance into action. Be open to receiving help.

741

The angels are with you, and your positive energy allows them to help you in miraculous ways.

742

Have faith, and continue on this path that is supported by the angelic realm. The angels want to help you with every aspect of your daily life—call upon them often.

743

The angels and ascended masters applaud you for your courage, and your commitment to following your Divine guidance.

744

The archangels and the angelic realm congratulate you on following your Divinely guided path. They're here to help you whenever you need them.

745

The angels want you to know you're on the perfect path to make changes in this situation—keep going! Your ideas for making changes are inspired.

746

The angels say that the steps you're taking are putting you on the right path toward ensuring that all your needs are met. The angels are with you, loving and helping you.

747

Your strong connection to the angelic realm has helped you to be firmly on the right path. Stay confident and centered as you progress.

748

You've been talking and listening to the "Angels of Abundance," who are now bringing you a floodgate of blessings and prosperity.

749

You've been talking and listening to the "Angels of Abundance," who are now bringing you a floodgate of blessings and prosperity.

The angels completely support you in manifesting your Divine life purpose. You're in the good habit of calling upon them, as well as being open to receiving their blessings and miracles.

750

Congratulations on making the decision to improve your life! God is watching over you and protecting you, especially during this time of transition.

751

The changes you're making are Divinely inspired by your positive thoughts and affirmations. Visualize this transition as smooth and harmonious, and your path continues to be peaceful.

752

Continue to have faith as you make these transformations and changes. You're doing the right thing, and your path is illuminated with Heaven's love and blessings.

753

You're making appropriate changes to improve your life. The ascended masters are helping you all along the way.

754

The archangels support your path, and they ask you to continue allowing the transformations that are emerging. Everything is changing for the better.

755

You're going through major changes right now that are putting you on the right path. Out of these changes, only good will come.

756

The changes that you're making help you manifest on a higher level, ensuring that all of your needs are met.

757

You're improving your life and putting yourself on the right path by making much-needed changes. Keep up the good work!

758

This transformation and change is the right direction for you to take in order to manifest abundance and prosperity.

759

You're on the correct path of preparation for your Divine life purpose. As you go through these changes, look for opportunities to help and teach others.

760

God is guiding your actions to help answer your prayers. The Creator ensures that all of your needs are met, now and in the future.

761

All of your needs are met as you continue with your positive intentions, thoughts, and affirmations. Your thoughts create your wonderful new reality.

762

Your faith in your new path is well founded. Give any material concerns to Heaven, and trust that your needs are met in miraculous ways.

763

The ascended masters applaud the path you've chosen, and they're ensuring that you're well taken care of along the way. Give them your fears, and ask them for help often.

764

The angels want you to know that there's nothing to fear or worry about. You're doing the right thing, and they're helping you along this path.

765

The change that you're going through is for the best, and your life is improving in many ways because of the actions you're taking. Your needs are met during and after this transition.

766

Trust that you've made the right choice, and that your needs are supplied by Heaven's blessings and your Divinely guided actions. All is well.

767

You're on the right path to increasing the flow of supply in your life. Stay centered, and focus on your desires and intentions.

768

Congratulations! Your Divinely guided actions have helped you overcome material limitations, and have ensured your financial security.

769

You're now manifesting everything you need for your Divine life purpose. Continue following your guidance, and all of your needs are supplied along the way.

770

You're working in perfect harmony with God and the Universe. You're to be congratulated on listening to your inner truth, and taking action accordingly. You're a powerful Lightworker!

771

Your positive outlook, affirmations, and optimism create Divine magic in your life. You're inspiring others with your loving light.

772

Your willingness to trust your Divine guidance is rewarded by miracles and manifestations coming your way. Continue to walk in faith, as you're on the right path.

773

This spiritual path you're on is fully supported by the ascended masters. You're making a wonderful difference in the world.

774

The angels say that you're on the right path, and ask you to keep up the good work. They're working with you to heal, teach, and manifest.

775

Congratulations on your willingness to change and improve your life. This is a wonderful transition that's bringing great blessings to you and others.

776

You're on the right path, and everything is going well for you. Surrender any remaining worries or cares—especially material concerns—to Heaven. You deserve to be completely happy.

777

Congratulations! You've listened well to your Divine guidance and have put that wisdom into fruitful action. You're now reaping the rewards. Your success is inspiring and helping others, so please keep up the good work.

778

Your willingness to listen to and follow your inner wisdom brings you great financial rewards, as well as other forms of prosperity. Be willing to receive, and pass along these gifts to others as you feel guided.

779

You're correct about your Divine life purpose, and you're taking the appropriate action. Keep going, and dive right into your mission without delay or hesitation.

780

Your financial security is assured as you continue devoting yourself to God and your spiritual path. Give any money worries to God for healing and manifesting.

781

Your positive thoughts and intentions are abundantly supplying you with everything you need.

782

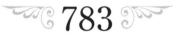

Your strong faith, coupled with the actions you're taking, make all your dreams come true. Abundance, in every sense of the word, is yours.

783

The ascended masters guide you along the right path. Keep listening to and following their guidance, and prosper in all ways.

784

The angels support the direction you've chosen in this situation. They're helping you realize all your dreams, including spiritual, financial, and emotional ones.

785

You've made the right choices about changing your life for the better. This new path brings you riches beyond your wildest dreams.

786

Congratulations! You've let go of your old ways of dealing with money, and have learned how to manifest abundance with your spiritual power.

787

You've set your sights clearly upon your goals and intentions. Keep going on this right path, as it's bringing beautiful treasures into your life.

788

Your bright light, positive intentions, and guided actions have struck gold. Through the spiritual law of cause and effect, you've attracted great riches.

789

You're on the right path for your Divine life purpose. You and your purpose are financially supported by Heaven's love.

790

God is watching over and helping your Divine mission, ensuring that you take the right steps.

791

Keep your thoughts positive and your heart open, as you're on the right path for your Divine life mission.

792

Your ideas, thoughts, and beliefs about your Divine life mission are correct. Keep your faith strong about yourself and your purpose.

793

You've been accurately hearing and following the Divine guidance given to you by the ascended masters. This has put you on the right path for your life mission.

794

The archangels and angels ensure that you're taking the right course of action for your Divine life purpose.

795

You've made the right changes to ensure the fruition of your Divine life mission.

796

Have no worries about your needs getting met. You're taking the right actions for your Divine life purpose, and Heaven makes sure that you're adequately supplied and supported along the way.

797

Heaven applauds you for fully committing to your Divine life purpose. You're on the right path.

798

All the doors are open for you, spiritually, financially, emotionally, and so on. This is because you've been listening to and following Divine guidance about your mission in life.

799

You've got a very important and much-needed life purpose. Your ideas and actions about your mission are correct—keep going!

800

God and the Universe abundantly support you and help to manifest your dreams into reality. Give any money worries to God for healing and manifestation.

801

Your prayers, positive thoughts, affirmations, and visualizations have been heard and answered by God and the Universe. You're receiving your wishes in wonderful and miraculous ways.

802

Continue to have faith that God's loving power is the Source of all the riches you need and desire. You're abundantly loved and cared for.

803

God and the ascended masters ensure that you have the money and other material support that you need. You're secure in all ways.

804

God and the angels bring new windfalls of abundance to you. You're fully supported by Heaven in all ways.

805

The changes that you're considering or experiencing are Divinely guided, and they help you to be more financially secure.

806

God helps you manifest financial security. Give any material concerns to the Creator, and be open to receiving miraculous help.

807

You're on the right spiritual path to manifest everything you desire. Have frequent conversations with God about your hopes, desires, needs, fears—in other words, *everything*. Heaven is helping you in all ways.

808

As you've placed God at the center of your thoughts, feelings, and actions, your Divine love ensures that all of the riches of Heaven and Earth support you.

809

God is supplying all the money and material support you need for your Divine life purpose. Keep your focus on giving service through your mission. The Creator is taking care of everything else.

810

Your positive thoughts and prayerful, meditative connection with God have opened the floodgates of abundance for you. Enjoy the miracles and blessings coming your way!

811

Your positive expectations, combined with your creative ideas and actions, bring you financial windfalls in wonderfully unexpected ways.

812

Continue your affirmations for abundance, as they're making your dreams a reality. Keep believing in miracles.

813

Your optimism about your finances is well founded, as the ascended masters ensure that you're supported and supplied for. Stay positive, and continue to follow your Divine guidance.

814

You're fully supported by the love of the angels, as well as by the positive affirmations you've been using.

815

This current change is the catalyst bringing your abundance to you. Stay positive and optimistic, and know that all is well.

816

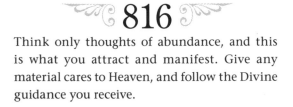

Think only thoughts of abundance, and this is what you attract and manifest. Give any material cares to Heaven, and follow the Divine guidance you receive.

817

Your path is abundantly supported and supplied because of your work with positive affirmations. Keep up the great work!

818

Your finances are healed and helped by your positive affirmations. Affirm: "I am financially secure now," and "I have a surplus of money to spare and share."

819

You have good reason to feel optimistic and positive about your Divine life mission, as it's fully supported and manifested by Heaven. Everything you need for your mission is given to you.

820

Your deep faith in God keeps you connected with the bountiful supply that's available to all of God's children. Ask and you shall receive.

821

Consistent work with positive intentions and affirmations is bringing you abundance in all ways. Expect miracles.

822

You have very powerful faith, which is a magical secret for manifesting. Stay centered in this faith, as it's tapping you in to the Universal power.

823

Your faith in the ascended masters' love and power has opened the doors for prosperity for you.

824

Your faith, coupled with the angels' love, brings you financial abundance.

825

The positive shifts you made in your financial beliefs and thoughts have allowed the flow of abundance to come more readily to you.

826

Have faith that all your material and financial needs are met, easily and harmoniously. Your beliefs create your reality, so only think about your desires and not your fears.

827

Have faith that you're on the right path, and that you're fully supported in all ways.

828

Your strong beliefs ensure a bountiful harvest of plenty for you and your loved ones. Keep the faith!

829

Trust that your financial needs are met as you devote time and energy to your Divine life mission.

830

Your practice of prayer, meditation, and quiet time has allowed you to Divinely connect with God and the ascended masters, who supply you with amazing abundance.

831

You've been following the Divine guidance given to you by the ascended masters. This has helped you elevate your consciousness to a positive and loving level, which attracts wonderful riches to you in all ways.

832

Keep the faith that the ascended masters have heard and answered your prayers, especially about your material needs. Trust and believe, as all is well.

833

The ascended masters are with you, paving the way for all your dreams to come true. Call upon them often, and be open to their help, as it arrives in wondrous ways.

834

The angels and ascended masters bring profound levels of abundance to you. Delight in the joy of Heaven's love for you!

835

The change that you're making or considering is Divinely guided by the ascended masters. This change allows more abundance to come your way.

836

The ascended masters have heard and answered your prayers for financial and material support. Your needs are well supplied, now and always.

837

You've accurately heard and are following the ascended masters' guidance. All the time, money, and information you need is supplied to you along the way.

838

The ascended masters bring you the money and other supplies you desire. Keep your spiritual focus at the center of your thoughts and actions, and all your needs are met.

839

The ascended masters ensure that you have everything you need for the fruition of your Divine life mission.

840

It's the sacred honor and pleasure of God and the angels to provide for you and your loved ones in all ways. Keep listening to and following your Divine guidance to access abundance.

841

The angels and your positive affirmations help you manifest abundance in every area of your life.

842

Have faith in the angels' loving power to answer your prayers. Be open to receiving the bountiful miracles they're bringing you.

843

The angels and ascended masters help manifest your prosperity. Ask them for help, and be open to receiving their blessings and miracles.

844

The archangels and angels surround you with blessings, and infinitely meet your every need.

845

You've been following the angels' guidance about making positive changes, which have opened the doors of abundance in your life.

846

Keep asking the angels to help you meet your needs. They're happy to supply for you and support you in all ways—financially, spiritually, physically, and emotionally.

847

You're on the right path with your work with the angels. Enjoy the blessings of abundance they're bringing to you.

848

As you ask the angels to help your finances, and are open to receiving their help and guidance, your prosperity is assured.

849

The angels make sure that you have enough money and other supplies to support your Divine life purpose.

850

The changes that you're making, or are considering, are inspired and fully supported by God.

851

Keep up your positive thoughts and affirmations, as they're fueling a big improvement in your financial flow.

852

Have faith that the changes you're making attract abundance into your life. This change is strengthening and healing you and your life.

853

The ascended masters guide and support you through this important change. Call upon them often for help, and be open to receiving their blessings and miracles.

854

You're following the angels' guidance about improving your life. The angels support you in all ways during and after this change.

855

You're dramatically changing the way in which you deal with money. Your new spiritual outlook has magnetized your manifesting power so that you attract abundance quickly and easily.

856

You've let go of old beliefs about money in favor of positive intentions, affirmations, and expectations. These changes allow you to attract unlimited abundance into your life.

857

You're on the right path with the changes you're making, and financial prosperity is among the rewards that you're receiving.

858

Windfalls of abundance are manifested by this change that you're making or considering. The change is a good idea!

859

The changes that you're making help you manifest all your needs and supplies for your Divine life purpose. You're supplied with all the money, time, and information you need for your purpose.

860

Your material and financial needs are abundantly supplied by God, as you give any financial concerns to the Source, and are open to hearing and following the guidance that follows.

861

Your positive thoughts are the key to attracting your financial abundance. Keep your mind focused on your desires, and don't direct any energy to thoughts of fear or worry.

862

Your faith and positive expectations create a magnetic force field that attracts abundance into your life. Your optimism is plentifully rewarded.

863

The ascended masters help supply you with everything you need. Ask them for assistance, and they can help you even more.

864

As you release old financial fears to the angels, they're able to bring you unlimited abundance sent to you straight from Heaven.

865

You've followed your Divine guidance about holding positive expectations, and as a result, you're reaping abundant rewards.

866

Release financial concerns to the Source of all, and be open to noticing and receiving the abundant supply of guidance and resources that Heaven is sending you right now.

867

You're on the right path of holding positive thoughts and intentions about your financial flow. Your intentions are now manifesting right before your eyes.

868

Your gratitude and appreciation for the many blessings in your life creates a magical energy that attracts amazing abundance to you.

869

Your needs are met, and your bills are paid as you focus on your Divine life purpose. Don't delay your purpose, awaiting more money. Dive in right now!

870

God and the Universe congratulate you for having the courage to commit fully to following your Divine guidance. The gratitude and riches of Heaven are bestowed upon you.

871

You've learned how to master your thoughts so that they're focused only on your desires and not on your fears. Because of this, you're consciously and rapidly attracting and manifesting your desires.

872

Continue to have faith in yourself and your path, and trust that you're fully supported in all ways.

873

You've accurately heard the Divine wisdom of the ascended masters, and it's leading you along the right path. The masters ensure that your needs are abundantly supplied.

874

The angels have successfully taught you to gather and use your spiritual power to manifest your dreams. Focus fully upon your desires—spiritual, emotional, financial, and so forth. Know that you deserve to realize all of them.

875

The changes you're making have put you on the right path for manifesting abundance in all ways.

876

You're on the right path of thinking about health, peace, abundance, and all that you truly desire. In this way, you ensure that you attract only from a place of love, and not from fear.

877

Well done! You've learned the secret of manifesting great abundance. Keep up the good work, and share it with others as you feel guided.

878

Your path is surrounded with great abundance. The more you notice the many gifts that life is giving you, the more your supply is amplified abundantly. The Universe loves a grateful recipient!

879

Yes, it's correct for you to dive into your Divine life mission right now. Your purpose is the right path for you and helps you manifest everything that's important to you.

880

God is surrounding you with abundant blessings and miracles. Enjoy them, as the Source loves to give.

881

Your positive thoughts and visualizations have manifested abundance for you in powerful ways. Keep focusing upon your desires, and visualize them as already being manifested.

882

Your supreme faith has magnetized a wealth of opportunities, experiences, and support to you. You're a powerful Lightworker!

883

You're operating as a team with the ascended masters. Your combined power creates magnificent examples of the Universe's generosity and abundance.

884

The angels joyfully bring you abundance and prosperity. Keep up your connection with the angelic realm, for they love you very much.

885

Your financial picture is changing for the better as you take guided action to improve your life. Know that you deserve health, wealth, and happiness—we all do!

886

Enjoy the abundant flow that's coming to you, and know that your needs are met now and in the future. Let go of any remaining material concerns, and enjoy feeling financially secure.

887

You're on the right path to manifesting great wealth. Keep your thoughts and heart centered on love and gratitude, and you'll continue to be abundantly cared for.

888

The Universe is abundant and generous, and you've learned how to step into the shower of its ever-present flow. Great financial prosperity is yours, now and in the future.

889

Your Divine life purpose is abundantly supported by the Universe. You have enough money, time, information, and material supplies to fully devote yourself to your mission.

890

God is supporting you and your Divine life mission with all the financial, energetic, intellectual and other resources you need. Ask and be willing to receive.

891

Your positive thoughts and affirmations concerning your Divine purpose have magnetized a wealth of opportunities and assistance. Be willing to receive these blessings, as the more you receive help, the more you can help others.

892

Have faith that your Divine life mission will always financially support you. You attract and manifest that which you have faith in.

893

The ascended masters ensure that you have everything you need to support your beautiful and Divine life purpose. Ask them for help with all matters related to your mission, and be open to receiving their assistance.

894

You have a wealth of physical and spiritual resources available to support your Divine life purpose. Call upon this help, and notice the miracles that come to you as ideas, inspiration, and direct intervention.

895

The doors of opportunity and abundance open for you right and left, especially concerning your Divine life purpose. The changes you're experiencing are signs of the increased support that the Universe bestows upon you and your mission.

896

Your Divine life purpose is fully supported by the Universe. As you focus upon your mission and release all cares to the Universe, everything flows to you abundantly.

# 897

You're on the correct path with your Divine life purpose, and everything you need is infinitely supplied to you right now.

# 898

Everything your heart desires is supplied to you, as you devote your focus, time, and energy to serving others through your Divine life purpose.

# 899

You have an important life purpose that is much needed in the world. This mission involves your natural talents, interests, and passions. All you need to do is use your gifts in service to others, and your needs are abundantly supplied in exchange.

900

Your Divine life purpose is fully and abundantly supported by God and the Universe. Ask and you shall receive.

901

Keep God and your positive intentions at the core of your Divine life purpose. Your prayers and meditations with the Creator ensure that your mission is highly effective in all ways.

902

Have faith in the Source's power to support every aspect of your Divine mission. Your faith magnetizes everything you need for your life purpose.

903

God and the ascended masters support you and your beautiful Divine life purpose. Ask them for any help you may need, and then be open to receiving.

904

Your Divine life purpose is powerfully supported by God and the angels. They're with you every step of the way.

905

The change that you're experiencing or considering is guided and fully supported by God. This change helps your Divine mission to unfold and manifest.

906

God is supplying any material needs you have for your Divine life purpose. You're safe and secure as you focus upon service.

907

God fully supports the course you're taking with your Divine life purpose. Everything that's ahead of you is bathed in God's golden light.

908

God is ensuring that your needs are abundantly supplied as you fully address your Divine life purpose.

909

Keep Heaven fully in the center of your Divine life purpose. Talk to God about every aspect of your mission, and listen with an open mind and heart to the loving guidance that comes to you.

910

God is helping you elevate your thoughts and consciousness about your Divine life purpose. Focus on Spirit, love, and service, and the material takes care of itself.

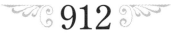

911

Your thoughts are manifesting into reality at an ever-quickening pace. Keep your thoughts about your Divine life purpose, focused only upon your desires, and give any worries or doubts to Heaven for transmutation.

912

The more you keep your thoughts and feelings dialed into faith, belief, and positive energy, the more your Divine life mission manifests in miraculous ways.

913

The ascended masters, especially the goddesses, are helping with your Divine purpose. They ask you to keep your thoughts and words voiced in the positive to help manifest the highest aspects of your mission.

914

The angels assist you in staying positively focused on your mission in life. Call on the archangels and angels for help with any question or need, especially as they relate to your purpose.

915

Your spiritual power and gifts are growing stronger as you continue to make Heavenly guided changes. Your strength and these changes are very important to the manifestation of your Divine purpose.

916

As you give cares and worries about your Divine life purpose to Spirit, everything opens up and is supplied for you. Your thoughts about your mission are manifesting into form rapidly, so focus only upon that which you desire.

917

You're on the right path with your Divine life purpose. Your thoughts and affirmations have a big impact on your purpose, so pay close attention to them and keep them focused on the positive.

918

Focus on "How may I serve?" using your natural talents, passions, and interests, and the material needs take care of themselves.

919

Your Divine life mission is manifesting rapidly, thanks to your positive thoughts, affirmations, and visualizations. Keep affirming that your desires transform into reality!

920

You have faith that you and your purpose are fully supported by God. Ask the Creator for whatever support you need for your purpose, and it's given to you in miraculous ways.

921

Keep believing in yourself and your Divine life mission. You have an important purpose, and you're qualified to fulfill it completely.

922

Your deep faith is magically manifesting important aspects of your Divine life purpose. Think of all the gifts and miracles you've received so far, and have faith that they'll continue, especially as it concerns your mission.

923

Have faith in the power of the ascended masters. They watch over you and fully support your sacred mission.

924

Angels surround you and your Divine life purpose with healing and supportive energy. Believe in yourself, your mission, and the angels. Trust that everything is in Divine and perfect order, now and always.

925

Stay optimistic about the changes you're experiencing, as they're an important part of your sacred mission in life. Your faith brings miracles into your life, and supports your purpose.

926

Have faith that everything you need for your Divine life purpose is supplied to you, now and in the future. Your faith opens the doorway for Spirit to bring you material support.

927

Keep believing in yourself and your dreams. This belief gives you the energy and the manifesting power for your Divine life purpose.

928

Trust that you'll continue to have every resource you need for your Divine life purpose. The Universe is fully supportive of you and your mission, now and in the future.

929

Your Divine mission in life is much needed, and helps others in important ways. Believe in your ability to carry this purpose to fruition, and it is done.

930

God and the ascended masters guide and support you and your sacred mission every step of the way.

931

Your positive thoughts and your prayerful conversations with the ascended masters open new doors of opportunity for your Divine dreams and purpose.

932

Continue to have faith in the guidance you're receiving from the ascended masters about your Divine life purpose.

933

The ascended masters love, support, and guide your Divine life purpose. Call upon them for help with any aspect of your mission.

934

The angels and ascended masters urge you to focus fully upon your Divine life purpose, and leave all material concerns to them.

935

The ascended masters fully support and guide the changes that you're making, which allow you to focus upon your Divine life purpose.

936

The ascended masters supply all your material needs while you focus on your sacred mission in life. Ask them for help with all aspects of your purpose, and be open to receiving their guidance and miracles.

937

You're accurately listening to and following the ascended masters' Divine guidance about your sacred purpose. They're helping you and your mission in all ways. Ask and you shall receive.

938

Keep listening to the guidance of the ascended masters, as they're helping you manifest a meaningful career with financial abundance, which fulfills your Divine life purpose.

939

Your Divine life purpose involves the ascended masters. They're behind the scenes, helping you along the way. You may be called to teach about them as well.

940

Your continued meditations and connections with God and the angelic realm give you complete guidance and support for your Divine mission.

941

The angels ask you to hold positive thoughts about yourself and your purpose. Know that you're qualified and ready to help others in an important way.

942

Your deep faith in the angels' ability to guide and support your Divine life purpose is opening new doors of opportunity for you. Keep believing!

943

Your Divine life purpose is blessed by the archangels, angels, and ascended masters. Ask them for help with your purpose, and be open to their assistance, which comes through guidance, signs, and miracles.

944

Your beautiful and important Divine life purpose is watched over and fully supported by the angels and archangels.

945

The angels guide and support the changes you're making, which enable you to fully focus upon your Divine life purpose.

946

The angels ensure that all your needs are met while you work on your sacred mission. Give material concerns to the angels for healing and manifestation.

947

Congratulations! You're on the right path for your Divine purpose, and the angels bless, guide, and support you and your mission.

948

You and the angels manifest great abundance to support your Divine life purpose. Be open to receiving everything you need that allows you to fully focus upon your mission.

949

The angels are fully committed to helping you with every aspect of your Divine life purpose. Work with them on your mission, as they are your teammates.

950

The changes that you're experiencing are Divinely guided and supported by God. They prepare you for a deeper and more exciting aspect of your sacred mission.

951

The changes and improvements that you're making open new opportunities and levels for your Divine purpose. Stay positive, and keep affirming your desires.

952

Have faith in the changes you're making, as they enable you to be more focused on your sacred mission in life.

953

The ascended masters Divinely guide the changes you're making to assist you with the fruition of your important purpose.

954

You're helped and guided by the angels through changes and transitions that prepare you for new aspects of your life purpose. The timing of these changes is Divine.

955

You're going through an intense period of change and preparation that enables you to take your Divine life purpose to an even higher level of sacred service.

956

As you go through this time of change, all your needs are supplied and supported by Spirit. Place all your focus on your Divine purpose, and give any material concerns to Heaven.

957

You're on the right path with the changes you're making. They open you to new information and energy that supports your Divine life purpose.

958

Congratulations on making the decision and having the courage to change your life so that you can fully focus upon your sacred mission! These new changes also open you to increased financial flow.

959

Continue to make whatever changes are necessary to allow yourself the time and energy for your Divine life purpose. These changes, and your mission, are fully supported by Spirit.

960

God is ensuring that everything you need for your Divine mission is supplied. Give any material concerns to Heaven, and be open to receiving.

961

Your thoughts about your sacred purpose are manifesting at a rapid rate, so be sure to keep them positive. Use affirmations to manifest whatever you need for your mission.

962

Have faith that all your needs are supplied as you devote yourself to your Divine purpose. Your faith magnetizes and manifests at a steady supply, now and in the future.

963

The ascended masters stand next to you, ready to assist you with every aspect of your sacred purpose. Ask them to send you whatever you need for your mission, and it is done.

964

The angels supply your material needs, while you focus fully upon giving service through your talents, interests, and passions. This is the heart of your Divine life mission, and it's blessed by the angels.

965

Know that the changes you're experiencing open new doors of opportunity, which further support you and your mission in life.

966

Give any material concerns to Spirit, and move forward on the Divine path of your mission. Keep your thoughts Heavenward, and the material world takes care of itself.

967

You're on the right path for your Divine life mission, so there's no need for worry or concern about meeting your material desires. Spirit is supporting and supplying everything you need, so you can fully focus upon bringing more light into the world with your talents, passions, and interests.

968

It's safe for you to receive all the abundance that the Universe is offering to you right now, especially because these are new opportunities for you to express your Divine life mission. Give all material concerns to Spirit.

969

Devote yourself to your sacred purpose right now, and trust that the money and material supply is always there to support you. Your mission is needed at this time, so please don't delay or procrastinate.

970

You're on the right path for your Divine life mission, and every aspect of your purpose is supported and guided by God.

971

You have every reason to be optimistic and hopeful about the path you're on, because it's illuminated with the light of your Divine life purpose. Keep affirming that your dreams are coming true, because they are.

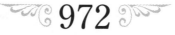

972

Believe in yourself and your power to bring more light into the world with your Divine life mission. Your faith opens doors for you and your purpose.

973

The ascended masters applaud and support the path you're on, as it's the path of your Divine life purpose. Keep working with the masters to manifest everything you need for your mission.

974

The angels are with you, guiding the wonderful path you're on, and helping you fully manifest your sacred mission. Call upon them for answers and support.

975

The changes you're experiencing are part of the preparation for, and the manifestation of, your Divine life purpose. Everything is in perfect order.

976

You're on the right path for your Divine life purpose, and your material needs are provided for along the way. You're safe and secure.

977

Congratulations! You've fully devoted yourself to your Divine life purpose, and your crystal-clear commitment has opened wonderful doors of opportunities for you. Walk through them with joy and confidence.

978

You're accurately hearing and following your Divine guidance about your sacred mission, and you're showered with spiritual, financial, and emotional rewards. Enjoy!

979

You're a shining example of someone who is courageously following their inner guidance successfully. You help many people, and will soon help even more. Please keep up the good work!

980

You've struck gold, spiritually and materially, through your willingness to trust and follow the guidance that God gives you. All the riches of Heaven support you and your purpose.

981

Your positive thoughts and affirmations ensure a steady financial flow from the work you do related to your Divine life purpose. Keep affirming your heart's desires.

982

Have faith that you'll always be financially secure as you fully devote yourself to your Divine life purpose. Your faith manifests your prosperity.

983

The ascended masters support you and your Divine life purpose with infinite abundance, to ensure that your needs are met while you devote yourself to sacred service.

984

The angelic realm helps you to be financially secure as you work on your Divine mission. Call upon the angels often, and be open to receiving their help.

985

Your financial flow is improving and increasing, helping you to more fully devote yourself to your sacred purpose.

986

As you let go of material concerns and worries, money that supports your Divine life purpose is more able to flow freely into your life. Give your cares to Spirit, and focus solely upon the giving of sacred service.

987

You're on the right path, both for your Divine life purpose and for your financial prosperity. You're in the flow of giving and receiving with gratitude and joy.

988

Your willingness to give of service through your Divine life purpose has blasted open the gates of Heavenly riches. Your mission is a wonderful demonstration of the universal law of giving and receiving.

989

Your financial security is assured as you fully devote yourself to following your soul's calling of sacred service.

990

God is calling upon you to focus on your Divine mission right now. You and your purpose serve an important function that's much needed in the world. You're ready and qualified to fulfill this function.

991

Keep your thoughts about yourself and your purpose at a high level of truth, love, and hope. See past any illusions of problems or lack, and know that everything is already healed and manifested in truth.

992

Believe in yourself and your mission. Your faith fuels the energy and commitment you need to see your Divine life purpose through.

993

The ascended masters ask you to fully devote yourself to your Divine life mission. They're with you, helping you with every aspect of your purpose. Ask and you shall receive.

994

The angels and archangels are with you, urging you to use your time and energy in sacred service. The angels give you Divine guidance about your next steps. Listen to them and follow in confidence.

995

The changes you're making create positive shifts for you, which help you more fully express and manifest your Divine life purpose. Ask for and be open to receiving help from Spirit along the way.

996

Give any material concerns to Spirit, and fully embark on your Divine life purpose. All your needs are met along the way.

997

The Universe applauds and supports your devotion to sacred service through your Divine life purpose. You're on the right path—keep up the good work!

998

You have a powerful and much-needed life mission. As long as you're working on this purpose, your flow of abundance is assured.

999

Get to work, Lightworker! The world needs your Divine life purpose right now. Fully embark upon your sacred mission without delay or hesitation.

* * *

BLESSINGS AND GRATITUDE TO THE FOLLOWING INDIVIDUALS . . .

. . . from Doreen Virtue:

Thank you to God, Jesus, the archangels, Hermes/Thoth/Merlin, and Pythagoras for your teachings and guidance.

Thank you to Louise L. Hay, Reid Tracy, Jill Kramer, Christy Salinas, Amy Gingery, Marius Michael-George, Steven Farmer, Lynnette Brown, and to everyone whom I've given angel-number readings.

. . . from Lynnette Brown:

Thank you to God, the angels, ascended masters, the wizards of the Divine realms, Melchizedek, Merlin, Thoth, Pythagoras, and Einstein for your incredible guidance, love, and support.

To my family, Jay, Nick, and Tom for all you do. Special thanks to my beloved Ryan and Claire for being willing to support me on this path and where it takes me. Despite the miles apart, I will always be with you because you truly have my heart.

Much gratitude to Doreen Virtue for all the lifetimes of opportunities, lessons, friendship, and fun. It has been, and continues to be, a great experience.

Heartfelt thanks to my friends, who laughed, cried, believed, and supported me during the birthing of this project, the "Psychic Fab Five," Angie and Duke Hartfield, the Thompson girls, Chris Marmes, Judith Lukomski, Radleigh Valentine, and my ATP family. Dreams really do come true!

✳✳✳　✳✳✳

ABOUT THE AUTHORS

Doreen Virtue, Ph.D. is a fourth-generation meta-physician and clairvoyant doctor of psychology who works with the angelic, elemental, and ascended-master realms. Doreen is the author of numerous best-selling books and products, including the *Healing with the Angels* book, where the angels' interpretations of the numbers first appeared. She's been featured on *Oprah*, CNN, *Good Morning America,* and in newspapers and magazines worldwide. Doreen teaches classes related to her books and frequently gives audience angel readings related to the meanings of numbers. For information on her products, workshops, message-board community, or to receive her free monthly e-newsletter, please visit: **www.angeltherapy.com**.

Lynnette Brown is an internationally known psychic, angel therapy practitioner, medium, and Reiki master who uses her Divine connections to the angelic and spiritual realms to channel information for healing and guidance. Lynnette is a speaker, teacher, Divine mystic, and spiritual alchemist. She facilitates workshops nationwide on angelic numerology, chakras, intuitive development, spiritual empowerment, healing with dolphins and whales, and living the life of your dreams. She's also the author of *Chakra Energy Oracle Cards* and the upcoming book *Angels in Hawaii.* She lives in Laguna Beach, California. Visit her Website at: **www. angelicwonders.com,** or write to her at P.O. Box 4947, Laguna Beach, CA 92652.

Photos of Doreen and Lynnette: **www.photographybycheryl.com**

NOTES

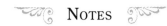

NOTES

We hope you enjoyed this Hay House book.
If you would like to receive a free catalogue featuring
additional Hay House books and products, or if you would
like information about the Hay Foundation, please contact:

Hay House UK Ltd,
Unit 62, Canalot Studios 222 Kensal Rd, London W10 5BN
Phone: 44-20-8962-1230 Fax: 44-20-8962-1239
www.hayhouse.co.uk

Published and distributed in the United States by:
Hay House, Inc. • P.O. Box 5100 • Carlsbad, CA 92018-5100
Phone: (760) 431-7695 or (800) 654-5126
Fax: (760) 431-6948 or (800) 650-5115
www.hayhouse.com

Published and distributed in Australia by:
Hay House Australia, Ltd. • 18/36 Ralph St. • Alexandria
NSW 2015 • Phone: 612-9669-4299 • Fax: 612-9669-4144
www.hayhouse.com.au

***Published and distributed in the Republic of
South Africa by:***
Hay House SA (Pty), Ltd. • P.O. Box 990 • Witkoppen 2068
Phone/Fax: 27 11-706 6612 • orders@psdprom.co.za

Distributed in Canada by:
Raincoast • 9050 Shaughnessy St. • Vancouver, B.C. V6P
6E5 • Phone: (604) 323-7100 • Fax: (604) 323-2600

Sign up via the Hay House UK website to receive the Hay
House online newsletter and stay informed about what's
going on with your favourite authors. You'll receive
bimonthly announcements about: Discounts and Offers,
Special Events, Product Highlights, Free Excerpts,
Giveaways, and more!